CORPORATE GOVERNANCE
Contemporary Issues and Challenges

CORPORATE GOVERNANCE

Contemporary Issues and Challenges

Edited by:

P. V. SARMA
S. RAJANI

KANISHKA PUBLISHERS, DISTRIBUTORS
NEW DELHI-110 002

KANISHKA PUBLISHERS, DISTRIBUTORS
4697/5-21 A, Ansari Road, Daryaganj
New Delhi-110 002
Phones : 2327 0497, 2328 8285
Fax : 011-2328 8285
e-mail: kanishka_publishing@yahoo.co.in

First Published 2007

ISBN 978-81-7391-970-1

PRINTED IN INDIA

Published by Madan Sachdeva for Kanishka Publishers, Distributors, 4697/5-21A, Ansari Road, Daryaganj, New Delhi-110 002, Typeset by Sunshine Graphics, Delhi, and Printed at Nice Printing Press, Delhi.

Preface

We take pleasure in stating that this book is a collection of the papers presented in a UGC sponsored National Seminar on "Corporate Governance: For Building Global Competence."

Corporate Governance, a phrase that not long ago meant little to all, but a handful of scholars and stakeholders has now taken center-stage across boardrooms around the world. Corporate governance deals with laws, procedures, practices and rules that determine a Company's ability to take managerial decisions vis-a-vis its claimants—in particular, its shareholders, creditors, customers, state and employees. The ultimate objective of corporate governance is to maximize long-term shareholder value. Increasing size of the firms, increased role of financial intermediaries and institutional investors in fund raising, increased complexities in the process of capital allocation, increased vulnerability of companies to market forces due to intensified competition and finally the most important—increased awareness among the stakeholders has led to greater levels of accountability and responsibility and have become the underlying reasons for increased attention to corporate governance in India.

The current corporate governance assessment for India has found that over the last few years a series of regulatory and legal reforms have transformed the Indian corporate governance framework and improved the levels of accountability and responsibility of insiders, fairness in the treatment of minority shareholders, Board practices and transparency. However enforcement and implementation of law and regulation remain important challenges. Corporations need to be transformed into a corporate community with self-regulation rather than external control. Corporation must pledge to honour their obligation to society by becoming economic, intellectual and social assets to each nation and community in which they operate.

In this context, it has been felt that a seminar on this topic would provide a platform for intellectuals from different sectors both academic and industry, to come together and deliberate on issues relating to corporate governance and its role in building global competitiveness among industries. The theme has been received well and there has been a good level of participation in the Seminar. Senior level executives from reputed organizations and eminent academicians shared their views and experiences on the occasion. The articles published in this book are select articles from among those presented in the Seminar. Some of them have been appropriately edited to avoid repetition. We thank all the authors for their valuable contributions.

We are grateful to the Management of Gayatri Vidya Parishad College for Degree and PG Courses. Our special thanks to the faculty of the Department of Management Studies for their help in organizing the Seminar.

We thank the University Grants Commission, New Delhi for sponsoring the Seminar and also funding the publication of this book. Last but not the least we thank the publishers, Kanishka Publishers for taking up the publication of this book.

Editors

Contents

List of Contributors

Saravana Kumar	Training Manager, ING Vysa Life Insurance, Viskhapatnam.
Dr. R. Vijaya	Director, AQJ Centre for PG Studies, Visakhapatnam.
N. Santosh Ranganath	Lecturer, Department of Commerce and Management Studies, Andhra University Campus, Etcherla, Srikakulam.
D. Naga Mani	Lecturer, Department of Commerce and Management Studies, Andhra University Campus, Etcherla, Srikakulam.
Kameshwar Rao	Asst. Prof., Al-Ameer College for Engg., Visakhapatnam.
Dr. R. Satya Raju	Ph.D. Professor, Department of Commerce and Management Studies, Andhra University, Visakhapatnam.
Rajesh Sashittal	Chief Manager, Regional Office, State Bank of Hyderabad, Visakhapatnam.
Dr. P. Viswanadham	Associate Professor (Finance and Accounting), Department of Commerce and Management Studies, Andhra University, Viskhapatinam (A.P.).
Mrs.Y. L. Lavanya	Research Scholar, Department of Commerce and Management Studies, Andhra University, Viskhapatinam (A.P.)
Mr. M. Vijay Kumar	Research Scholar, Department of Commerce and Management Studies, Andhra University, Visakhapatnam, (A.P.).

A. U. Durga Devi	Reader in Commerce, St. Theresa's Autonomous Degree College, Eluru.
P. M. Soundharyam	Lecturer in Commerce, St. Theresa's Autonomous Degree College, Eluru.
Dr. S. S. Prasada Rao	Associate Professor, College of Mgt. Studies, GITAM, Visakhapatnam.
G. V. S. Sekhar	Associate Professor, College of Mgt. Studies, GITAM, Visakhapatnam.
Samshuddin Sheik	Associate Professor, College of Mgt. Studies, GITAM, Visakhapatnam.
Prof. P. V. Sarma	Professor and Director, School of Management Studies, G.V.P.College for Degree and PG Courses, Gayatri Valley, Visakhapatnam.
T. V. V. Phani Kumar	Asst. Professor, School of Management Studies, G.V.P.College for Degree and PG Courses, Gayatri Valley, Visakhapatnam.
Prof. S. Rajani	Head of the Department of Management Studies, Gayatri Vidya Parishad College for Degree and PG Courses, Visakhapatnam.
Mrs. D. Jyotsna Rani	Asst. Professor, Mallareddy College of Secunderabad.
Prof. J. V. Prabhakara Rao	Principal, College of Arts and Commerce, Andhra University, Visakhapatnam.
Dr. S. Rajani	Head of the Department, Gayatri College for Degree and P.G. Courses, Visakhapatnam.
P. V. Rao	Associate Professor, Department of Management Studies, G.V.P. College of Engg., Visakhapatnam.
P. Pinakapani & Dr. K.S. Bose	Associate Prof., School of Mgt. Studies, G.V.P. College for Degree and PG Courses, Gayatri Valley, Visakhapatnam.
M. S. R. Seshagiri	Assistant Professor, Department of MBA, GVP College for Degree and PG Courses.

Dr. B. Madhukar	Senior Lecturer, Department of MBA, G.V.P. College for Degree and PG courses.
Dr. B. Madhukar	Sr. Lecturer, G.V.P. College for Degree & PG Courses, Visakhapatnam.
Smt. P.V. Mohini	Asst. Prof., G.V.P. College for Degree & PG Courses, Visakhapatnam.
V. V. Ajith Kumar	Faculty Member, ICFAI National College, Visakhapatnam.
K. V. V. Murali Someswara Rao	Faculty, Gayatri Vidya Parishad College for Degree and PG Courses, Rushikonda, Visakhapatnam.
Prof. B. Appa Rao	Director-Center for Banking Studies and Research, Department of Commerce and Management Studies, AU, Visakhapatnam.
Rumki Benerjee	Faculty Member, Institute of Technology and Management, Warangal.
K. Nageswara Rao	Lecturer in Commerce, SVSS Arts and Science College, Attilli, WG Dt.
G. Srinivasa Rao	Asst. Prof. and HOD, Department of Management Studies, Samata College, Visakhapatnam.

1

Challenges and Issues Pertaining to Corporate Governance

Saravana Kumar

Corporate governance has taken centre-stage across boardrooms around the world. The term applies to all aspects of a business. Given the fact that technology is expected to play a key role in helping organizations achieve their business objectives, it is imperative to discuss the role of corporate governance over technology.

Although "Corporate Governance" still remains an ambiguous and misunderstood phrase, three aspects are distinctly evident.

- First, there is no unique structure of Corporate Governance in the developed world; not is one particular type unambiguously better than others. Thus, one cannot design a code of corporate governance for Indian companies by mechanically importing one form or another.
- Second, Indian companies, banks and Financial Institutes (FIs) can no longer afford to ignore better corporate practices. As India gets integrated in the world market, Indian as well as international investors will demand greater disclosure, more transparent explanation for major divisions and better shareholder value.
- Third, corporate governance goes far beyond company law. The quantity, quality and frequency of financial and managerial disclosure, the extent to which the board of directors exercise their fiduciary responsibilities towards shareholders, the quality of information that management share with their boards, and the commitment to run transparent companies that maximize long-term shareholder

value cannot be legislated at any level of detail. In fact, these evolve due to the volatile role played by the more progressive elements within the corporate sector and thus, enhance corporate transparency and responsibility.

Corporate Governance deals with laws, procedures, practices and rules that determine a Company's ability to take managerial decisions vis-à-vis its claimants – in particular, its shareholders, creditors, customers, the State and employees. There is a global consensus about the objective of good corporate governance

maximizing long-term shareholder value

The current corporate governance assessment for India has found that over the last few years, a series of legal and regulatory reforms have transformed the Indian corporate governance framework and improved the level of responsibility and accountability of insiders, fairness in the treatment of minority shareholders and stakeholders, board practices and transparency. Nonetheless, *enforcement and implementation of law and regulations remain important challenges.*

The challenge for regulators is to enhance market integrity by enforcing rules and regulations in a professional, timely, transparent and consistent fashion. Regulators should ensure that *sanctions and enforcement* are credible deterrents to help align business practices with the legal and regulatory framework, in particular with respect to related party transactions and insider trading. This would greatly improve confidence of investors and other stakeholders in the financial markets.

The current institutional framework places the oversight of listed companies partly with the Department of Company Affairs (DCA), partly with the Securities and Exchange Board of India (SEBI) and partly with the stock exchanges. This fragmented structure gives rise to regulatory overlap and weakens enforcement. A *streamlined regulatory structure* would help improve accountability and market discipline.

Challenge—1

Board Practices in India Need to be Strengthened

A key missing ingredient in India today is a strong focus on *director professionalism*. Directors are expected to know their duties of care and loyalty to the company and all shareholders. However, as that is not always the case, we believe that the law or other regulations should clearly spell out the responsibilities of directors and they themselves should engage in the formulation of their tasks and work procedures.

- Board practices need not mean to adopt the German system of two-tier boards to ensure desirable corporate governance. A single board, if it performs well, can maximize long-term shareholder value.
- The position of director of a company is an eternally critical one which can bring a cataclysmic change in the governance of that Company. The role of the corporate board of directors as stewards of their shareholders and stakeholders has internationally gained significant ground in recent decades. This is the reason why, no single person should hold directorships in more than 10 listed companies as it would arise for conflict of interests among all the companies which this person holds directorships for.
- For non-executive directors to play a material role in corporate decision-making and maximizing long-term shareholder value they need to:
  - become active participants in boards rather than passive advisors.
  - have clearly defined responsibilities within the board such as the Audit Committee.
  - stop reappointing any director who has not attended a certain minimum attendance criterion fixed for the meetings.

The recommendation in this field calls for a greater role and influence for non-executive *independent* directors, a tighter delineation of independence criteria and minimization of interest-conflict potential, and some stringent punitive punishments for executive directors of companies failing to comply with listing and other requirements.

Also that the shareholders and stakeholders of the company appointing them as their executives should have the benefit of their full attention and accordingly, has suggested some limitations on the nature and number of their other directorships.

Challenge—2

Interested Shareholders

Shareholder democracy, like many other lofty principles of fair play and public policy, is often supported more in precept than observed in practice. In order to strengthen the democratic rights of minority shareholders, it may be desirable that matters directly affecting their interests are decided upon exclusively by them without brute majority of numbers having full sway.

Accordingly, one of the most important recommendations is the concept of *interested shareholders* who would be required to abstain from voting on specified matters that impact upon *some but not all* the shareholders. This is somewhat analogous to, but not the same as, the principle of *interested directors* being required (as part of their fiduciary responsibility) not to participate in or vote upon resolutions they are interested in. Conscious of the potential of such a measure being abused.

It is recommended that this privilege be limited to a few specific matters and even there with suitable provisions for breaking stalemate situations.

Challenge—3

Measures Promoting Transparency and Informed Shareholder Participation

A related issue of equal importance is the need to bring about greater levels of informed attendance and meaningful participation by shareholders in matters relating to their companies.

The recommendations addressing this issue relate to more meaningful and transparent accounting and reporting, improved annual reports concomitant with more detailed filing with regulatory authorities and greater facilitation for informed participation using the advances in converging information and communications technologies.

Under additional shareholder's information, listed companies should give data on:

1. High and low monthly averages of share prices in a major

stock exchange where the company is listed for the reported year.

2. Greater detail on business segments up to 10 per cent of turnover, giving share in sales revenue, review of operations, analysis of markets and future prospects.

Challenge—4

Corporate Social Responsibility

Accountability to stakeholders is a continuing topic of divergent views in corporate governance debates. In line with the developing trends towards an integrated model of governance, it is recommended to emphasize corporate social responsiveness and ethical business practices, seeking what might well turn out to be not only the first small steps for better governance on this front but also the promise of a more transparent and internationally respected Corporate India of the future.

Challenge—5

Impact of Foreign Direct Investment

We are conscious of proposals running the risk of criticism that they would be inimical to the general policy of welcoming foreign direct investment in an environment of economic liberalization. It must however be appreciated that the kind of level and transparent business relationships that corporations seek to develop with their investors does come at a cost, whether it is in their home country or in the host country. Foreign Investment however though will also bring in the policies and framework of rules followed in the investors' country which might again have a conflict of interest for Indian business scenario or other issues formerly discussed.

Challenge—6

Business Continuity Planning/Disaster Recovery Planning

Every organization faces the risk of having to deal with known and unknown disasters. Organizations that use IT strategically and need to recover from significant business interruptions deploy Business Continuity Planning and Disaster Recovery Planning System. BCP should not be documented but also tested, updated and validated regularly to mitigate the threat of the non-availability of IT services disrupting automated operations and key business operations. BCP/DRP are not only about infrastructure and planning, they are also about people. People play a key role in ensuring that the organization continues to function securely at pre-determined acceptable levels. DRP/BCP are like insurance and need to be renewed as insurance is done with premium payments.

Challenge—7

Performance Management

Business, you can drive it or be driven. In a business context, risk is not just about disasters and security attacks, but also about the business risks of costly project failures. Given the significant costs and strategic value of industries like manufacturing and IT, measuring its performance is as important as any other key business function. Yet many organizations find performance measurement challenging, so they settle for measuring what they can rather than what they want or need to. Assessment and analysis of every unit used in the entire business machine should be done in terms of its performance and its productivity. Lack of any correct performance measurement systems among businesses would lead to a HR disaster and might result in a fall in morale and fun in case of employees and might become stale and insipid in cases of other business units.

Challenge—8

Information Security and Data Integrity

Security related incident have been on the front burner of organizations for several years. Security breaches may occur due to the negligence of staffers, third-party access to key applications, or lack of appropriate security of information systems. It is essential that all organizations have information security policies and procedures in place as well as a formal incident response management team that can detect and escalate security breaches. Key risk areas that need to be focused in logical access management include lack of procedures on user access rights and inadequate review of access rights on a periodic basis. Segregation of duties amongst users should be addressed to promote tighter control. Physical access risks exist on account of poor awareness levels and training. Investments made by organizations are for physical goods and not assets especially data. Physical security functions are typical not integrated with information systems security.

Data integrity risk encompasses all of the risks associated with the authorization, completeness and accuracy of transaction as they are entered into, processed by, summarized and reported on by various application systems deployed by an organization. These risks pervasively apply to each and every aspect of an application system used in supporting a business process. Integrity can be lost due to programming and processing errors and poor management. Adequate preventive controls and detections need to be put in place to ensure that only valid and complete data are entered in to all systems and applications.

Rules of Corporate Governance cannot be static. It must be reviewed. Simply put, corporate governance refers to an economic, legal and institutional environment that allows companies diversify, grow, restructure and exit and do everything necessary to maximize long-term shareholder value. Thus, non-executive directors and disclosures are parts, and not the whole, of corporate governance. To most international experts on the subject, corporate governance is interplay between companies, shareholders, creditors, capital markets, financial sector institutions and company law. Hence, a code of corporate governance must attempt to address all these issues and challenges.

Nevertheless, it is vital for the corporate well-being of India. To appreciate this, it is useful to take a peep at the vision of the near future. It is a vision that will almost certainly come to bear, and shall shape tomorrow's corporate governance:

1. First, a larger number of foreign portfolio investors will constantly raise their demand for better corporate governance, more transparency and greater disclosure. This is precisely what happened in US from the early 80s and in Britain since the early 90s.
2. Second, in a year or at most two there will be the entry of foreign pension funds. Since these funds tend to hold on to their stocks longer than mutual funds, their fund managers will be even more active in insisting upon better corporate governance.
3. In the foreseeable future, there could conceivably be, least half a dozen private equity or leveraged buy-out funds, each with an investment base of US $50 million or more. These

funds will take a two to three-year view on under performing but asset rich Indian companies, take them over, de-list for couple of years, and then return to the market to exit from their portfolio after successful turnaround. Thus, Indian companies will become targets for take-over. The targets becomes all the more attractive if management has not given long-term shareholder value.

4. Indian Financial Institutions will not continue to support management irrespective of performance. Therefore, one will see FIs converting their outstanding debt to equity and setting up Mergers and Acquisitions subsidiaries to sell their shares in under performing companies to more dynamic entrepreneurs and managerial groups.
5. Financial press will get stronger than ever before. In the last five years, the press and financial analysts have induced a level of disclosure that was inconceivable a decade ago. This will increase and force companies to become transparent – not just in their financial statements but also in matters relating to internal governance.

Finally, when India has full capital account convertibility, an Indian investor who has money to invest would have the option of investing either in an Indian or a foreign company. The investor would be inclined to invest in the Indian company if it follows some stands or transparency, disclosure and Corporate Governance.

I intend to touch upon various other challenges like Corporate Citizenship, Social Responsiveness, Capital Market Issues, Creditors Rights, Voting and Listing Procedures but, for paucity of space, I am refraining myself to do so.

REFERENCES

1. "Desirable Corporate Governance", A Code, Address by N.Kumar, President CII, April 1998.
2. "Report on corporate excellence on a sustained basis", Address by Dr. M. R. Rao, Director, IIIMB.
3. "Global Edge and Corporate Governance", Lecture by Sri Kumar Mangalam Birla, Davos Summit, 2004.
4. "Information Technology and Corporate Governance", valedictory address, Sunil R. Chandiramani, Earnst and Young, 2005.

2

Corporate Governance in India

Dr. R. Vijaya

Corporate Governance is the system by which Organizations are directed and controlled. The Corporate Governance Structure specifies the distribution of rights and responsibilities among different participants in the Corporation, such as board, managers, shareholders and other stakeholders and spells out the rules and procedures for making decisions on corporate affairs. By doing this, it also provides the structure through which the company objectives are set and the means of attaining those objectives and monitoring performance.

- Organization for Economic Co-operation and Development (OECD).

  The system by which Companies are directed and controlled, thus placing the Board of Directors of a Company in the centre of the governance system is Corporate Governance.

- Cadbury Committee.

Corporate Governance refers to the relationship among owners, directors and managers. While in the broader view Corporate Governance can be defined as a set of systems and processes which ensure that a company is managed in the best interests of all the stakeholders. Stakeholders mean not only the shareholders but also the employees, creditors, customers, bankers, suppliers and society (Kumara Mangalam Birla Committee).

Cadbury Committee Report

The movement of corporate governance has been activated with the publication of the Cadbury Committee Report.

The Cadbury Committee was set up in the UK in May 1991 under the Chairmanship of Sir Adrian Cadbury, Former Chairman Cadbury Schweppes by the Financial Reporting Council, the London Stock Exchange and accountancy profession for reviewing the aspect of corporate governance related to financial reporting and accountability. The objective of this was to help raise the standards of corporate governance and the level of confidence in financial reporting and auditing by setting out clearly what it sees as the respective responsibilities of those involved and what it believes is expected of them. The Committee submitted a 19-point report and code of best practices in December 1992. The report laid stress upon the role of Board of Directors, duties of the board and its composition, role of the non-executive directors, the directors emoluments, the accounting practices and principles, the effectiveness of internal control system and the need of auditors to act with due care. The Committee stressed upon setting up of 'audit committees' for efficiency of 'cultural audit' in companies.

The committee stipulated that all major investment and disinvestments proposals, changes in financial and marketing structure, important appointments and findings of the internal auditors, have to be presented, discussed and approved by the Board of Directors. The Board should be briefed periodically on the progress of various projects of the company under implementation. Transparency, being the hallmark of corporate governance, it must be issued that no vital information is concealed from the board. The Committee also felt that in the interest of corporate democracy, there should be separation of power at the top level. There should be a balance of power and authority so that no individual enjoys unfettered power of decision-making. The Committee stated that directors are primarily responsible for maintaining adequate accounting records and the accuracy of such records depends on the prevalence of a sound system of internal control. The Committee further emphasized that the companies must make compliance statements and the compliance itself is a matter between the board and their shareholders.

Kumara Mangalam Birla Committee Report

A Committee on Corporate Governance was set up on May 7 1999, by the SEBI under the Chairmanship of Sri Kumar Mangalam Birla, member SEBI Board, to promote and raise the standards of Corporate

Governance. It recognized that financial reporting and disclosure which are also related to the accounting policies of a company and the existing accounting standards and auditing practices, are cornerstones of Corporate Governance.

The Committee on Corporate Governance considered the following critical issues having a bearing on the quality of financial reporting.

- Consolidation of accounts of subsidiaries.
- Segment reporting where a company has multiple lines of business.
- Disclosure and treatment of related party transactions.
- Treatment of deferred taxation.

In the opinion of the Committee, the imperative for corporate governance lies not merely in drafting a code of corporate governance, but in practising it. Even now, some companies are following exemplary practices, without the existence of formal guidelines in this subject. Structures and rules are important because they provide a framework which will encourage and enforce good governance, but these alone cannot raise the standards of corporate governance. What counts is the way in which these are put to use. The Committee has framed the codes of Corporate Governance and has also suggested the implementation of the code through stock exchange. In the event of default on Corporate governance compliance, the Committee has recommended for the delisting of such companies by the stock exchange. Two types of recommendations – mandatory and non-mandatory – are being suggested by the Committee.

Mandatory Recommendations

- For strengthening the norms of listing agreements, the companies must strictly comply with the new listing norms. The stock exchanges must be given more powers to penalize the defaulting companies.
- Companies with a capital of Rs. 10 crore and net worth of Rs. 25 crore should comply with the corporate governance code by April 2000. Companies with capital of Rs. 5 crore should comply with the listed norm by April 2001.
- The Board should meet at least four times a year.

- The Committee recommends setting up of an Audit Committee having 3 non-executive directors, majority of them being independent.
- The K.M. Birla Committee has mooted the independence of the Board of Directors. Persons of caliber should be inducted as independent directors and they must be capable of making positive and quality contributions to the company.
- A person can become a director in a maximum of 10 companies and would be restricted to 5 companies if he is the chairman of the said company.
- The Board should delegate its power of share transfer to share transfer agents/Registrar.
- The disclosure of Quarterly Reports by companies should be Mandatory. Half-yearly reports should be sent compulsorily to all shareholders.
- The Committee has also suggested the use of postal ballot system in critical matters like change of company's name, objectives, sale, corporate restructuring and further issue of shares through preferential allotment.

Non-mandatory Recommendations

Financial institutions or investment institutions are not permitted into the Board except in case of a default or a potential default. The code has tried to keep the FIs at an arms length so that they are not privy to unpublished price sensitive information.

Corporate Governance—The Indian Scenario

It would be beyond controversy if one says that there is a strong need for raising the general standard of corporate governance in India. Shareholders in India are scattered, mute and frequently obliged to managements for dividends and petty gifts offered at the annual general body meetings. They give their consent obligingly to all resolutions enabling the management to fulfill their vested interests. There is a lack of accountability and transparency in an average Indian Company. In a survey it was found that though family shareholding accounts merely 3.3 per cent of aggregate paid up capital in big business, surprisingly the management of these companies gives priority to interest of such controlling minority at the cost of long-run interests of the company and its majority shareholders.

The structure of corporate governance in India is in a very bad shape. Stories of accounting juggleries, siphoning of funds, investing and selling off associate companies and subsidiaries, benefits to promoters at the cost of other shareholders, etc., are not uncommon. The culprits are not necessarily over the night operators; names of blue-chips often appear in these stories. In India, companies were managed on the basis of family ties and managers could get away with poor corporate governance due to laxity of shareholders. Financial Institutions were totally ineffective in demanding better standard of corporate governance and others were too small and spread out to put any pressure.

Despite the dire need for high standards of corporate governance the corporate behaviour in India continues to deviate from the expectations. As many as 2500 of 3900 companies listed between 1991 and 1996 have completely disappeared without any published information. More than 100 dot companies floated in India have vanished and a number of non banking finance companies have run away with hard earned money of the investors. Some of the directors of a well-known telecom equipment manufacturer of Punjab (with 49% government stake) lead the company to bankruptcy eating away even the salaries and the Provident Fund of the employees. An industrial survey revealed that hardly 11 per cent of the directors of Boards of running textile mills had any knowledge of the Industry.

There are many companies which are not paying adequate attention to the basic procedures for shareholders' service; for example, many of these companies do not pay adequate attention to redress investors' grievances such as delay in transfer of shares, delay in dispatch of share certificates and dividend warrants, and non-receipt of dividend warrants; companies also do not pay sufficient attention to timely dissemination of information to investors as also the quality of such information. The SEBI has been regularly receiving large number of investor complaints on these matters. While enough laws exist to take care of many of these investor grievances, the implementation and inadequacy of penal provisions have left a lot to be desired.

The concept of corporate governance has been attracting public attention for quite sometime in India. The topic is slowly stepping out of the halls of academia and finding acceptance for its relevance and underlying importance in the Industry and capital markets. Some progressive Indian companies though very few have voluntarily established high standards of corporate governance.

To quote an instance, the ICICI has become the first financial institution to enforce its own brand of corporate governance through its nominee directors who are on the Boards of various companies. The ICICI Staff are being educated on the idea of what constitutes corporate governance.

In India a number of steps have already been taken by Securities and Exchange Board of India (SEBI) for strengthening Corporate Governance, some of which are:

- Strengthening of disclosure norms for Initial Public Offers.
- Providing information in director's report for utilization of funds and variation between projected and actual use of funds according to the requirements of the Companies Act.
- Inclusion of cash flow and funds flow statement in annual reports.
- Declaration of quarterly results.
- Mandatory appointment of compliance officer for monitoring the share transfer process and ensuring compliance with various rules and regulations.
- Timely disclosure of material and price sensitive information including details of all material events having a bearing on the performance of the company.
- Despatch of one copy of complete balance sheet to every household and abridged balance sheet to all shareholders.
- Issue of guidelines for preferential allotment at market related prices.
- Issue of regulations providing for a fair and transparent framework for takeovers and substantial acquisitions.

Lack of ethics in Indian Corporations is yet another blow to good corporate governance. Ethics play an important role in efficient corporate administration. It is well-known that most of the businessmen are lured by the fast-buck culture to earn as much money as fast as possible. Ends justify means to many of our Indian businessmen. An alarming number of frauds in Indian Corporates including public sector banks portray how unethical the Indian corporates are. Hundreds of such frauds have been detected in more than 15 banks including the giant public sector banks such as State Bank of India, Andhra Bank, Bank of India, Indian Overseas Bank, Union Bank of India and many more.

In addition to corruption deceptive advertisements, spurious products, unethical HR practices, Tax evasions, lack of pollution control have also become a part of bad governance in many Indian corporates.

This savvy state of affairs could no more exist. If only the recommendations of the Cadbury Committee and Kumara Mangalam Committee are put into practice it would enable Indian Corporates attain professional standards.

Globalization has brought in its wake increased global opportunities for the competent people, better choices for customers and increased opportunities for strategic alliances and collaborations, for the companies. The employees, the customers and business partners will all like to deal with those companies which are run professionally and are fair and transparent in their dealings. The public will prefer those companies which believe in business ethics and are socially committed. This points to the requirement of putting into practice good corporate governance principles.

The management is responsible for implementation of the policies and plans laid down by the Board and is accountable to the board. The management including the executive directors are critical to the success of any enterprise hence, the need to have management which is highly professional and committed.

Board of Directors

The most important body in the corporation sector is its Board of Directors. It is often said that the cause of Corporate governance is served depending on how well the Board of Directors of a company is organized and structured. The Kumara Mangalam Birla Committee on Corporate governance set up by the SEBI in its recommendation has highlighted the importance of the Board thus: Good Corporate governance dictates that the Board be comprised of individuals with certain personal characteristics and core competencies such as recognition of the importance of the Board's tasks, integrity, a sense of accountability, track record of achievements and the ability to ask tough questions. Besides having financial literacy, experience, leadership qualities and the ability to think strategically, the directors must show a significant degree of commitment to the company.

The Board of a company should have an optimum combination of executive and non-executive directors with not less than 50 per cent of Board comprising the non-executive directors. The number of independent directors would depend on the nature of the company. In case a company has a non-executive chairman, at least one-third of the Board should comprise of independent directors and in case a company has an executive Chairman at least half of the Board should be independent. The institutions should appoint nominees on the Boards of companies only on a selective basis where such appointment is pursuant to a right under loan agreements or where such appointment is considered necessary to protect the interests of the institution. The Chairman's role should in principle be different from that of the chief executive, though the same individual may perform both roles.

Regarding more powers for the Board; "The Board should retain... full and efficient control over the company and monitor the executive management."

Shareholders

Shareholders—the owners of the company have an active role to play to ensure good corporate governance. They should not consider annual general meetings as places to discuss the contents of the lunch packet or the petty gifts, which would be offered. In this respect more than the individual shareholders the institutional investors have a major role to play. Institutional investors who hold blocks of shares are in a much better position to foster professional management. United, they hold considerable voting rights in companies which they can use to block decisions they consider prejudicial to the company as a whole or even they can go to the extent of ousting inefficient governance.

Auditors

Auditors are the third constituents of corporate governance. "The central issue is to ensure that an appropriate relationship exists between the auditors and the management whose financial statements they are auditing. Shareholders require auditors to work with and not against the management while always remaining professionally objective—that is to say applying their professional skills impartially and retaining a critical detachment and consciousness of their accountability to those who formally appoint them. Maintaining this professional and objective relationship is the responsibility, both of the Board of Directors and of the Auditors." Auditors are often criticized to be working more for a company manager than for its shareholders. An independent Audit Committee should be set up by the Board of a company. This would go a long way in enhancing the credibility of the financial disclosures of a company and promoting transparency, which is one of the components of ideal corporate governance. The composition of the audit committee is based on the fundamental premise of independence and expertise.

- The audit committee should have a minimum of three members, all being non-executive directors with the majority being independent and with at least one director having financial and accounting knowledge.
- The chairman of the committee should be an independent director.
- The chairman should be present at the AGM to answer shareholder queries.

Disclosure and Transparency

The corporate governance framework should ensure that timely and accurate disclosure is made on all material matters regarding the corporation, including the financial situation, performance, ownership, and governance of the company. Disclosure helps improve public understanding of the structure and activities of enterprises, corporate policies and performance with respect to environmental and ethical standards, and companies' relationships with the communities in which they operate. Public disclosure is typically required, at a minimum, on an annual, or even more frequently in the case of material developments affecting the company. A strong disclosure regime is a pivotal feature of market-based monitoring of companies and is central to shareholders ability to exercise their voting rights. Disclosure can also be a powerful tool for influencing the behaviour of companies and for protecting investors. A strong disclosure regime can help to attract capital and maintain confidence in the capital markets. Shareholders and potential investors require access to regular, reliable and comparable information in sufficient detail for them to assess the stewardship of management, and make informed decisions about the valuation, ownership and voting of shares. Insufficient or unclear information may hamper the ability of the markets to function, may increase the cost of capital and result in a poor allocation of resources.

The guiding principles of good disclosure practices suggested by OECD are:

- Disclosure should include, but not be limited to, material information on:
  - *(a)* The financial and operating results of the company.
  - *(b)* Company Objectives.
  - *(c)* Major share ownership and voting rights.
  - *(d)* Members of the Board and key executives, and their remuneration.
  - *(e)* Material foreseeable risk factors.
  - *(f)* Material issues regarding employees and other stakeholders.
  - *(g)* Governance structures and policies.
- Information should be prepared, audited, and disclosed in accordance with high quality standards of accounting, financial and non-financial disclosure, and audit.
- An annual audit should be conducted by an independent auditor in order to provide an external and objective assurance on the way in which financial statements have been prepared and presented.
- Channels for disseminating information should provide for fair, timely and cost-efficient access to relevant information by users.

Social Responsibility

The scope and meaning of Social Responsibility of Business is no longer limited to philanthropy, which was practiced in the past with different motives in mind. This was generally prompted by the intention of making a good impression for publicity or for reducing the tax burden and sometimes, even undertaken as an exercise in conscience cleaning. The increased competitive pressure after opening up of the Indian economy associated with consumer awakening has changed the scene. Indian Business and Industry must realize that it can no longer get away with undesirable business practices. A strong consumer movement in any case will not allow substandard and poor quality products, blatant environmental degradation, shady financial dealings etc. In the present highly competitive environment it is not enough to only see that the company's operations enhance shareholders' value but the company must also show concern for other stakeholders i.e., consumers, suppliers, creditors, the bankers, employees, the government and society at large. Showing interest and involvement in the dominant social issues facing the community endears a company to the local community and public at large.

It is increasingly being realized now that better corporate governance and transparency results in enhancing the image of the company and thus improve its stock market capitalization. It therefore makes a better sense for business to be ethical in its dealings and functioning. In this post globalization era with MNCs and FDIs increasing it is inevitable for Indian Organization to incorporate good and ethical corporate governance.

3

Corporate Governance: Challenges and Issues

N. Santosh Ranganath and D. Naga Mani

Corporate governance refers to the manner in which corporation is directed, and laws and customs affecting that direction. It includes the laws governing the formation of firms; the by-laws established by the firm itself, and the structure of the firm. The corporate governance structure specifies the relations, and the distribution of rights and responsibilities, among primarily three groups of participants: the board of directors, managers and shareholders.

This system spells out the rules and procedures for making decisions on corporate affairs; it also provides the structure through which the company objectives are set, as well as the means of attaining and monitoring the performance of those objectives. The fundamental concern of corporate governance is directors and managers act in the interests of the firm and its shareholders, and to ensure the means by which managers are held accountable to capital providers for the use of assets. Issues of fiduciary duty and accountability are often discussed within the framework of corporate governance.

In the United States, a corporation is governed by a *board of directors*, which has the power to choose an executive officer, usually known as the *chief executive officer*. The CEO has broad power to manage the corporation on a daily basis, but needs to get board approval for certain major actions, such as hiring his/her immediate subordinates, raising money, acquiring another company, major capital expansions, or other expensive projects. Other duties of the board may include policy setting, decision-making, monitoring management's performance, or corporate control.

The board of directors is nominally selected by and responsible to the *shareholders*, but perverse incentives have pervaded many corporate boards in the developed world, with board members beholden to the chief executive whose actions they are intended to oversee. Most often members of the boards of directors are CEOs of other corporations, which some see as a conflict of interest. The concerns of shareholders over administration pay and stock losses periodically has led to more frequent calls for Corporate Governance reforms.

Corporate governance principles and codes have been developed in different countries and issued from stock exchanges, corporations, institutional investors, or associations of directors and managers with the support of governments and international organizations. As a rule, compliance with these governance recommendations is not mandated by law, although the codes linked to stock exchange listing requirements may have a coercive effect.

Corporate Governance is the relationship among various participants in determining the direction and performance of companies. The primary participants are Shareholders, Management and the Board of Directors.

Other participants include the employees, customers, suppliers, creditors and community. The concept of corporate governance has gained tremendous importance in the recent past, especially after the second half of 1996.

Main Activities of the Board and Top Management

- Create vision, mission values
- Devise group level strategy
- Build corporate identity
- Maintain cost of capital
- Government on behalf of shareholders
- Manage external environment
- Evaluate and reward business level performance
- Select and energize people
- Manage sharing and transfer of common resources
- Collect embed and disseminate knowledge

- Decide about strategic decisions of an enterprise
- Decide about organization structure, design and key process.

Corporate Governance—Competition, Emerging Markets

1. *Corporate governance* and a poor competitive environment in the affected countries.
2. Ownership is by far the exception in developing countries.
3. Fast long-term growth with different *governance* systems, in developed countries.
4. *Corporate financing* patterns in emerging markets in the 1990s were broadly similar to those observed in the 1980s. Unlike their counterparts in advanced countries, large developing countries firms continued to rely overwhelmingly on external sources to finance their growth of total assets.
5. Conglomerates are inefficient, financially precarious and necessarily create moral hazard. It also indicates that contrary to widely held beliefs, product market competition in emerging countries is no less intense than in advanced economies.

Main Reasons for the Upsurge of Corporate Governance

The recent interest about corporate Government is primarily a product of four factors.

Assertion of Rights by the shareholders.

(a) Significant presence of Foreign Institutional Investors.

(b) Awareness on the part of lending institution.

(c) Integration of India into the World Economy.

(d) Strong Media presence.

(e) Participants' involvement in Corporate Governance.

(f) Shareholders have not been able to fulfill the historic role effectively for the reasons that they are widely spread and many of them find it difficult to travel to the meeting place. But in the context of complex nature of modern business, the scope of areas requiring shareholders' approval has enlarged.

(g) The significant presence of foreign institutional investors

who demand greater professionalism in the management of Indian corporate has also led to the keen interest in the corporate Governance.

(h) There is awareness on the part of lending institutions which are now being subjected to rigorous accounting norms, particularly with regard to income rendition and provisions against non-performance loans so they are giving much more emphasis to good and efficient corporate governance.

Corporate Governance—Structure

The analysis of *corporate governance* structures in developing countries has long been hindered by a lack of detailed information. One benefit to arise from the Asian crisis and the focus of the international financial institutions on *governance* structures has been the assembling of a large body of evidence on *corporate governance* structures in developing countries at the World Bank. This has included information on the structure of share ownership and *corporate governance* laws. Thus, we are now in a position to construct a more informed picture of the *governance* structures in a wide range of developing countries.

Corporate Governance and Corporate Finance

Governance is most conducive to growth under certain historical circumstances, but not in others. Good *corporate governance* practices include the corporation's business behaviour in its operational environment. Investors are therefore guided as much by the financial statements as they are by the enterprise's business behaviour.

The construction industry has thus far escaped such scrutiny: however, many of its participants are being subjected to good *corporate governance* requirements. Governments and consumers too have due diligence expectations, much of which is being translated into statutory regulation. Regrettably, there has thus far not been a global holistic and proactive response from the construction industry as a whole. The development of globalisation with particular reference to the establishment of a common code of conduct, undertakes a review of the definition and evolution of good *corporate governance* and determines its current *status*, assesses construction industry practices against international good *corporate governance* standards, and proposes an enabling framework for the industry.

Good *corporate governance* practices extend beyond financial requirements to include the corporation's business behaviour in its operational environment. As an extension to this requirement, the operational environment, in good *corporate governance* terms, includes the corporation's social and environmental performance. Investors are therefore guided as much by the financial statements of an enterprise as they are by the enterprise's business behaviour. Consumers too are increasingly supporting those products that can demonstrably show an appropriate response by the enterprise to its operational environment. Increasingly consumers are avoiding products produced by enterprises that fail in performing due diligence in the *manufacturing* and marketing of those products.

With the exception of listed construction enterprises, the construction industry has thus far escaped such scrutiny, for a variety of reasons. However, many of its participants, such as investors, the workforce and material manufacturers are being subjected to good *corporate* governance requirements. Governments and consumers too have due .

Corporate Governance—Globalisation

Corporate governance and ethics and spirituality onto the global agenda. The second struggle – determining a management model – is playing out in global institutions such as the World Trade Organization, the United Nations, and the World Bank. Two of the major areas in which globalisation has a significant influence are economics and human rights.

Economics

The integration of world affairs has created a world economy that is inter-dependent and inter-connected. A prime example is the attack on the World Trade Centre: this event in a single modern state wiped millions of dollars off global stock values and continues to impact upon thousands of air travellers around the world. Yet another example of the extent of economic integration is the ability companies have to undertake and locate their work in different countries, either in whole or in part. This is largely due to information and communication technologies facilitating a virtual 24-hour workday.

Human Rights

The development of human rights is one of the areas that supports the anthropological view of globalisation: the history of the evolutionary process of human civilization is one in which the strengthening of individual rights, as opposed to group rights, is a definite trend. In more recent times, the ease and extent to which information is capable of being spread has increased awareness of global human behavioural patterns and quality of life. The global population is now more aware of what behaviour is acceptable and what is not, and who is enjoying what quality of life and where. As an example, internal resistance is increasing in countries and societies where women and children's rights are abused or non-existent.

Global Characteristics of Corporate Governance

Fundamental paradigm shift by all participants in the construction industry to enterprise development and management, a shift based solidly on probity and respect. The paper argues that such a commitment by industry participants could lead to an enabling environment for effective delivery and for growth, improved performance and continuous development of the industry. Good *corporate governance* is after all, about the values supporting excellence as well as the creation of an ethical culture.

Corporate governance is the process and structure used to direct and manage the business affairs of the company towards enhancing business prosperity and *corporate* accountability with the ultimate objective of realizing long-term shareholder value, whilst taking into account the interest of other stakeholders.

Relevance of Corporate Governance to Indian Context

There is a need to bring better corporate Government in India in the context of Liberalisation, Privatisation and Globalisation (LPG) of Indian economy. The following factors underline the relevance of corporate Government to Indian context.

(i) Indian Boards are not in tune with times.

(ii) Holders of limited stake determine the destiny of major shareholders.

(iii) Family feuds result on stalemate and confusion.

(iv) Changing business environment.

(v) Shift in Government attitude.

(vi) Vision development.

(vii) Brand building.

(viii) Competitive edge.

(ix) Professional managers and independent auditors did not help much.

Strategic management is the theme for survival for corporate in the present competitive environment. Strategic Management is depending on – clear understanding regarding company's mission, objectives and strategic, proper environment analysis and corporate analysis. Important issues in Corporate Governance are:

- Sound Management
- Fiduciary relationship
- Responsibility
- Accountability
- Return on Integrity

Confederation of Indian Industry issued many recommendations for Board of directors for efficient and effective performance in Corporate Governance for the Indian Industrial Development.

Conclusion

Corporate India needs to make giant steps in order to take the full advantage of globalisation and information technology. The leadership of the centre comprising of board of directors and top management would have to be truly processional and responsible. There should be code of corporate governance. The centre should focus more on their core activities like giving direction, vision, empowering others.

Business Body like CII should form a consensus on arriving at a code of corporate governance and ethical practices. Financial Institutions should insist on professionalisation and sound corporate governance for providing financial support to any organization. The rating agencies should give specific attention on corporate governance. The movement for better corporate governance is not just for the lending institutions or for investor protection, but, it is a movement for survival and growth of Corporates in the era of globalisation and liberalisation.

4

Corporate Governance Reporting

Kameshwar Rao

Introduction to Corporate Governance

Corporate Governance is the policies, procedures, and rules governing the relationships between the shareholders, directors and management of a company, as defined by the applicable laws, the corporate charter, the company bylaws, and formal policies. Primarily it is about managing top management, building in checks and balances to ensure that the senior executives pursue strategies that are in accordance with the corporate mission. It consists of a set of processes, customs, policies, laws and institutions affecting the way a corporation is directed, administered or controlled. Corporate Governance governs the relationships among the many players involved and the goals for which the corporation is governed. The principal players are the shareholders, management and the board of directors. Other stakeholders include employees, suppliers, customers, banks and other lenders, regulators, the environment and the community at large.

The Corporate Governance actually has multiple meanings, which includes:

- A legal meaning, depending on the country where a firm resides or operates,
- The processes by which companies are directed and controlled,
- Encouragement of company's compliance with codes,
- A field in economics, which studies the many issues arising from the separation of ownership and control,

- The framework of rules, relationships, systems and processes within and by which fiduciary authority is exercised and controlled in corporations.

Need for Corporate Governance Reporting

The last decade has seen profound changes in corporate financial reporting practices. This change is driven by:

- Additional disclosure requirements stipulated in revised and new accounting standards;
- Additional disclosure requirements prescribed through amendments to the Companies Act, 1956;
- Disclosure requirements under the various SEBI regulations;
- Recent focus on Corporate Governance Reporting.

Additional disclosure requirement is a response of regulators to investor's demand for better information, both in terms of quantity and quality. Statutory requirements set out the minimum information that companies should disclose. However, the companies, particularly large and highly admired publicly traded companies, have gone beyond those minimum requirements. Voluntary disclosure, Segment Reporting, Related Party Transactions, Global Reporting Initiative, Value Added Statements, Economic Value Added etc., are the recent trends in the reporting system. The changes have occurred not only in the information content of annual reports, but also in presentation. Large companies use the annual report as an effective channel for corporate communication. Therefore, it is not surprising to see continuous improvements in the presentation of annual reports. Corporate Governance Report has been emerged as a vital and essential one that must be prepared and presented by the companies.

SEBI code of Corporate Governance requires listed companies to include a separate section of "Corporate Governance" in their annual reports. This section should include a detailed compliance report on corporate governance. The code provides the following suggested list of items to be included in the report.

1. A brief statement on company's philosophy on code of governance.
2. *Board of Directors*:This should include the relevant information regarding the following...

- Composition and category of directors like promoter, executive, non-executive, independent non-executive, nominee director etc.
- Attendance of each director at the Board of Directors meeting and the last Annual General Meeting.
- Number of other Board of Directors or Board Committees he/she is a member or chair person of.
- Number of Board of Directors meeting held, along with the dates.

3. *Audit Committee*: This head shall disclose the following:
   - Brief description of terms of reference.
   - Composition, name of members and chairperson.
   - Meeting and attendance during the year.
4. *Remuneration Committee*: This should consist the vital information regarding the following:
   - Brief description of terms of reference.
   - Composition, name of members and chairperson.
   - Attendance during the year.
   - Remuneration policy.
   - Details of remuneration to all the directors, as per format in the main report.
5. *Shareholders Committee*: Information under this category shall include:
   - Number of non-executive director heading the committee.
   - Number of shareholders complaints received so far.
   - Number of problems not solved to the satisfaction of shareholders.
   - Number of pending share transfers.
6. *General Body Meeting*: This includes the information regarding:
   - Location and time, where last the Annual General Meetings held.

- Details of any special resolutions passed in the AGMs.
- Whether the special resolutions were put through postal ballot last year, details of voting pattern.
- Details of the person who conducted the postal ballot.
- Procedure for postal ballot.

7. *Disclosures*: This is a very important one as it envisages about the following:
   - Disclosures on materially significant related party transactions with its promoters, the directors or the management.
   - Details of non-compliance by the company, penalties imposed on the company by stock exchange or SEBI or any statutory authority, on any matter related to capital markets, during the last three years.
8. *Means of Communication*: This includes the information about:
   - Half-yearly report sent to each household of shareholders.
   - Quarterly results.
   - Which newspapers normally published in.
   - Any website, where displayed.
   - Whether it also displays official news releases.
   - The presentations made to institutional investors or to the analysts.
9. *General Shareholder information:* The information under this head shall include:
   - Annual General Meeting: Date, time and venue.
   - Financial calendar.
   - Date of book closure.
   - Dividend payment date.
   - Listing on stock exchanges.
   - Stock code.
   - Market price data: high, low during each month in the last financial year.

- Performance in comparison to broad-based indices such as BSE Sensex, CRISIL indes etc.
- Registrar and transfer Agents.
- Share Transfer System.
- Distribution of Shareholding.
- Dematerialization of shares and liquidity.
- Outstanding GDRs / ADRs / Warrents or any convertible instruments, conversion date and likely impact on equity.
- Plant locations.
- Address for correspondence.

With the introduction of the above Corporate Governance Reporting system by the SEBI, the investor has got an opportunity to have a better insight into the affairs of the company as it maintains a transparent way of revealing the most sought after financial information and norms governing the Board of Directors.

5

Trends in Corporate Governance

Dr. R. Satya Raju

In Corporate Governance practices, India can be considered one of the best in the world in following corporate governance practices. As a result of several failures in business organisations, the concept of corporate governance has become so popular during the recent period. This concept has gained a considerable currency of literature all over the world. Several organisations, including the World Bank are focussing their attention on this subject. It is included in several management courses, executive development programmes and some other educational programmes. The attention of OECD, the World Bank, International Monetary Fund, International Finance Corporation is very high on corporate governance to protect the interest of shareholders. The emphasis is on higher standards of transparency, accountability, discipline to enhance shareholders value. The World Bank concentrates its efforts on modernising the legal framework and strengthening the judicial system to promote economic and social development. The board's objectives of assistance are to help bring about legal and judicial reform, improve governance and physical infrastructure, and increase access to justice. Key elements of reforms include: promoting judicial independence through improved appointment systems, planning, and financing, as well as disciplinary procedures; modernising judicial administration and case management; and training judges and court personnel. Governance improvements encompass strengthening anti-corruption programmes, building capacity in public agencies and civil society organisations and supporting bar associations and legal education.

Research studies reveal lack of corporate governance in several organisations in India and abroad. As a result, there is an unexpected change in the corporate culture all over the globe. In India, about 1,400 companies were disappeared during 1991-96. Over one hundred dot.com companies were vanished from the Indian business. Several non-banking companies had also been closed down. Because of the huge investments, institutional investors can effectively use ownership rights and make a worthwhile contribution to governance of companies. The growth of institutional investors is very significant in the UK and USA. In 1963, individuals held 54 per cent of corporate equity and institutional investors 29 per cent. By 1994, the proportions were changed drastically to 20 per cent and 60 per cent respectively. More corporate democracy and better behaviour go a long way to improve the current business culture in the eyes of the public, but unless these changes are accompanied by a new vision of the purpose of business, they will be seen as mere palliatives.

The Institute of Company Secretaries of India (ICSI) one of the professional organisations defines, "Corporate Governance as the application of best management practices, compliance of law in true letter and spirit and adherence to ethical standards for effective management and distribution of wealth and discharge of social responsibility for sustainable development of all stakeholders." According to Confederation of Indian Industry (CII), corporate governance deals with the laws, procedures, practices, implicit that determine—a company's ability to take informed managerial decisions vis-à-vis its claimants, the shareholders, creditors, customers, employees and the state. As per the Cadbury Committee in the UK, the three pillars of corporate governance are – nomination committee, remuneration committee and audit committee. These committees have to perform various functions as directed. In Germany, the corporate governance system has two-tier Board structure—the Supervisory Board (SB) and the Executive Board (EB). In Japan, corporate governance emphasises growth and market share of the organisation.

The US corporate governance structure is stipulated by the legal system. The contents of the established corporate laws in each state are same containing a general committee of stakeholders and a board of directors. The stakeholders are the supreme rulers of the corporate governance because they have the power to appoint and dismiss members of the board of directors. In Germany, the legal characteristic of German corporate governance is having a dual structure based on the joint decision system. In German organisations, three functions, i.e., a general committee of stockholders, and auditor's committee and a board of directors are statutory bodies. The stockholders of Japanese organisations positioned as the supreme of corporate governance. They have powers to appoint and dismiss directors.

Corporate governance is very important in the present context of cross cultural environment. It helps for the following purposes: to practice ethics and values; to create confidence among the stakeholders; to improve operational efficiency of the business; to protect the rights of the shareholders; to provide protection to financial and other lending institutions; to strengthen the Board of Directors; to provide autonomy and responsibility to the Board of Directors; to create wealth and economic value.

Some Committees and Associations

The recommendations of various committees are highly useful for effective governance. Some of the committees are: The Cadbury Committee (1991) of UK. The Chairman – Sri Adrian Cadbury; The King Committee (1994) South Africa. The Chairman – Meriyn King; The Toronto Stock Exchange Report of Canadas (1994); Australian Association of Investment Managers (1995); OECD Principles of Corporate Governance; International Corporate Governance Network (1995); Centre for European Policy Studies, Brussels (1995); The Vienot Committee (1995); Davis Global Advisors Inc. (1996); The Blue Ribbon Committee of the USA; The Kumar Mangalam Birla Committee of India; Confederation of Indian Industry.

All these committees and associations studied the functioning of corporate governance in various countries and submitted reports with, several recommendations.

Several studies revealed that there was a need for restructuring and reforming the Boards in both public sector and private sectors. The shareholders value and other stakeholders interest was not protected fully. The national and international image and understanding on various global and local companies was low. The Boards were responsible for several scams and misappropriations. The checks and controls were not adequate for improving the systems. The government had not understood the real role of the

Board for effective management of the enterprises. The Boards could not take proper decisions due to the intervention of political or government representatives. The impact of the top management functioning in several organisations was low on positive side, high on negative perspective. The structure, systems and style of functioning of the Boards was not upto mark.

Experience at Global Level

The world's most admired companies or India's most respected companies have been following some well accepted norms and practices including corporate governance. At global level, General Electric, Microsoft, Coco-Cola, Intel, Berkshire Hathaway, IBM, Wal-Mart, Cisco Systems, Dell Computer, Merck, Lucent Technologies, AT & T, Pfizer, Sony, Ford Motor, Toyota Motor, Jhonson & Jhonson, P&G, American Express, Home Deport were considered to be the top twenty most admired companies. In India, as per the Business World study the top ten most respected companies were: Infosys, Hind Lever, Reliance Industries, Wipro, L&T, ITC, Dr. Reddy's Labs, Ranbaxy, Nestle India. Some parameters considered for rating these corporate enterprises were: Top Management or Boards, Quality of talent, ethical organisations; socially responsible organisation, customer satisfaction, steady corporate performance, good returns to shareholders and creating value for stakeholders.

OECD Principles

The OECD principles of Corporate Governance are highly relevant for management experts, financial consultants, investors, policy makers, corporate executives and administrators all over the globe. The principles issued by OECD in 1999 were revised in 2004 on corporate governance. The main reasons were that the corporate governance was identified as one of the pillars of the international financial architecture and because it has emerged as a powerful instrument with a wide range of applications for economic development policy and for public service reform.

The OECD Principles of Corporate Governance

Ensuring the Basis for an Effective Corporate Governance Framework

The corporate governance framework should promote transparent and efficient markets, be consistent with the rule of law and clearly articulate the division of responsibilities among different supervisory, regulatory and enforcement authorities.

The Rights of Shareholders and Key Ownership Functions

The corporate governance framework should protect and facilitate the exercise of shareholders' rights.

The Equitable Treatment of Shareholders

The corporate governance framework should ensure the equitable treatment of all shareholders, including minority and foreign shareholders. All shareholders should have the opportunity to obtain effective redress for violation of their rights.

The Role of Stakeholders in Corporate Governance

The corporate governance framework should recognise the rights of stakeholders established by law or through mutual agreements and encourage active co-operation between corporations and stakeholders in creating wealth, jobs, and the sustainability of financially sound enterprises.

Disclosure and Transparency

The corporate governance framework should ensure that timely and accurate disclosure is made on all material matters regarding the corporation, including the financial situation, performance, ownership, and governance of the company.

The Responsibilities of the Board

The corporate governance framework should ensure the strategic guidance of the company, the effective monitoring of management by the board, and the board's accountability to the company and the shareholders.

The Commonwealth already provides a well established and influential framework for policy review, and in this respect the particular advantages which the Commonwealth has to offer—both as a club of nations and as an organisation—are that member countries have: a similar structure and system of government, public administration and law; a similar structure and system of commerce–law, institutions, accounting, management and business practices; a common working language; and an organisational structure which enables governments and professional associations to regularly, meet, debate and develop common policies and ideas to promote a positive policy environment.

Corporate governance in the Commonwealth is important and is concerned with the profitability and efficiency of Commonwealth business enterprises, and their capacity to create wealth and employment; the long-term competitiveness of Commonwealth countries in the global market; the stability and credibility of the Commonwealth financial sectors, both nationally and internationally; the relationships between business enterprises within an economy and their sustained ability to participate in the global economy; and the relationship between such business enterprises and their various stakeholders comprising shareholders, managers, employees, customers, suppliers, labour unions, communities, providers of finance, etc.

Corporate governance is essential about leadership: leadership for efficiency; leadership for probity; leadership with responsibility; and leadership which is transparent and which is accountable.

The Guidelines Represent 16 Principles

As per them; the board should:

Principle 1 – exercise leadership, enterprise, integrity and judgement in directing the corporation so as to achieve continuing prosperity for the corporation and to act in the best interest of the business enterprise in a manner based on transparency, accountability and responsibility;

Principle 2 – ensure that through a managed and effective process board appointments are made that process board appointments are made that provide a mix of proficient directors, each of whom is able to add value and to bring independent judgement to bear on the decision-making process;

Principle 3 – determine the corporation's purpose and values, determine the strategy to achieve its purpose and to implement its values in order to ensure that it survives and thrives, and ensure that procedures and practices are in place that protect the corporation's assets and reputation;

Principle 4 – monitor and evaluate the implementation of strategies, policies, management performance criteria and business plans;

Principle 5 – ensure that the corporation complies with all relevant laws, regulations and codes of best business practice;

Principle 6 – ensure that the corporation communicates with shareholders and other stakeholders effectively;

Principle 7 – serve the legitimate interests of the shareholders of the corporation and account to them fully;

Principle 8 – identify the corporation's internal and external stakeholders and agree a policy, or policies, determining how the corporation should relate to them;

Principle 9 – ensure that no one person or a block of persons has unfettered power and that there is an appropriate balance of power and authority on the board which is, inter alia, usually reflected by separating the roles of the chief executive officer and Chairman, and by having a balance between executive and non-executive directors;

Principle 10 – regularly review processes and procedures to ensure the effectiveness of its internal systems of control, so that its decision – making capability and the accuracy of its reporting and financial results are maintained at a high level at all times;

Principle 11 – regularly assess its performance and effectiveness as a whole, and that of the individual directors, including the chief officer;

Principle 12 – appoint the chief executive officer and at lease participate in the appointment of senior management, ensure the motivation and protection of intellectual capital intrinsic to the corporation, ensure that there is adequate training in the corporation for management and employees, and a succession plan for senior management;

Principle 13 – ensure that all technology and systems used in the corporation are adequate to properly run the business and for it to remain a meaningful competitor;

Principle 14 – identify key risk areas and key performance indicators of the business enterprise and monitor these factors;

Principle 15 – ensure annually that the corporation will continue as a going concern for its next fiscal year.

Commonwealth Association

The Commonwealth Heads of Government Meeting (CHO GM) declaration of November 1997 was to establish 'The Commonwealth Association for Corporate Governance' (CACG) in 1998. The mission of the CACG is "promoting excellence in corporate governance in Commonwealth countries". This registered as a public society in

New Zealand and is supported by Shell Group, Government of New Zealand, ICSA, London and the Commonwealth Secretariat. It provided training and education in over 30 Commonwealth countries. The CACG conducts workshops on the good governance and the best practices. It has developed a range of courses or workshops on this programme. It also conducts a five-day CACG certification programme. It brought out several guidelines and established, Institute of Directors in Zambia; Papua, New Guinea and other countries. In 2002, CACG encouraged the University of South Pacific (USP) in Fizi to become an affiliate to conduct Company Directors Courses. Several Programmes were conducted to Directors and Cabinet Ministers on this subject. The CACG received a prestigious International Corporate Governance Network Award.

Indian Perspectives

In India, several companies are eager to have corporate governance. Some of them are examined in the following few paragraphs:

Infosys

The Board consists of 10 members. As per the by-laws of the company, the company can have upto 12 members in the board. The current board contains four independent directors and six executive directors and all the executive directors are the founders of the company.

The board has the following three committees: Audit Committee; Compensation Committee; Nomination Committee.

Non-executive directors constitute 40 per cent of the Board. The Board had divided the responsibility for the management of the company between executive chairman and CEO, and a managing director, President and COO, the non-executive directors and independent and accomplished professionals in the corporate and academic worlds.

The Infosys management is committed to global levels of transparency and disclosure. As per the recommendations of the Cadbury Committee, the management provided all the required information to the shareholders of the company.

Dr. Reddy's Labs

The Board represents 12 members. The board had met four times during the year 1997-98 with clear agenda. Non-executive directors had accomplished professionals in the corporate, academic and medical fields. Except for four Directors hold Directorship in more than 10 companies. Non-executive directors effectively took part in the Board meetings and were also regular in attending the meetings. All the required information was provided to the shareholders in the meetings. Key information on high and low share prices of the company has disclosed under the heading, shareholders information. Defaulters by debtors were discussed when they were written off. No loans were advanced to any of the directors. The company had not defaulted on any loan repayment, interest payment, statutory tax or levy. The economic value added of the company was favourable and indicated high profitability.

BSES

BSES is energy supplier company which has delivered much more than electricity to India. It had enhanced customer satisfaction with option levels of quality. The Board consists of nine members of which six are non-executive directors. The company continues to endeavour to follow the globally recognised best practices of governance. The company believes that strong and sound corporate governance practices would enable BSES to face the Challenges of growth effectively and successfully and contribute to enhancing shareholder value.

The institutional nominees on the Board of the company are professionals of considerable standing from very senior levels and all of them have substantial background in various disciplines like power industry, coal industry, insurance and project finance. They actively participate in the deliberations of the Board and attend Board meetings regularly. Nominee Directors function independently of their respective financial institutions. They are professionals of high standing and actively participate in the deliberations of the Board.

The company was among the first to appoint Audit Committee way back in May 1986 and has appointed a Compensation Committee of Directors. The accounts of the company are governed by various statutory enactments and are drawn in accordance with the generally accepted accounting standards. The company makes regular and timely disclosures of all material developments. The managements also reports to Financial Institutions on major developments as required under loan covenants. The company regularly holds Board meetings and at least one such meeting is held every month for which the agenda papers are normally circulated about a week in advance. The company continues to endeavour to adopt and follow the best practices of governance keeping the long-term interest of all stakeholders. The company has five committees known as: Audit Committee, Investment Committee, Share Committee, Compensation Committee, Environment Committee.

Asian Paints

Asian Paints (India) Limited is committed to good corporate governance. It believes that best board practices, transparent disclosures and empowerment of shareholders are necessary for creating shareholder value. In industry-wide corporate governance initiative in India was pioneered by the Confederation of Indian Industry (CII) in 1997-98. Subsequently, the Securities and Exchange Board of India (SEBI) set up a committee on corporate governance and based on the recommendations of this committee, a new Clause 49 has been inserted into the listing agreements of all the stock exchanges in the country. Clause 49 specifies the standards that Indian companies have to meet and the disclosures they have to make with regard to corporate governance.

The company's commitment to corporate governance precedes this statutory requirement. Asian Paints had set up an audit committee as far back as 1990 under the chairmanship of an independent director. Appropriate disclosures are made to the shareholders, thereby ensuring creator transparency and better financial reporting. As on 31 March 2002, the Board comprised of 14 Directors, out of whom, six are promoter-Directors. Three of the six promoter-Directors, including the Executive Chairman are whole-time Executive Directors, while the other three are Non-Executive. Of the remaining eight Directors, seven are Non-Executive and Independent and one is Non-executive but not Independent.

The Asian Paints Board met nine times during the year 2001-02. The Board meetings took place on 7 April, 2001, 6 June, 2001, 29 June, 2001, 23 July, 2001, 28 August, 2001, 30 October, 2001, 23 January, 2002, 7 February, 2002 and 8 March, 2002. The maximum gap between any two Board Meetings was 84 days.

The company does not have a remuneration committee. The Executive Chairman and other Executive Directors are paid remuneration as per their agreements with the company. These agreements are placed for approval before the board, shareholders and such other authorities as may be necessary. The remuneration structure of the Executive Chairman and other Executive Directors comprises salary, house allowance, commission, perquisities, contribution to provident fund/superannuation, gratuity and leave salary.

The Company has an independent audit committee. The composition, procedures, powers and role/functions of the audit committee constituted by the company comply with requirements of the Companies Act, 1956 as well as those of Clause 49 of the listing agreement.

CMC Limited

The company has made corporate governance a practice and a continuous process of development. The Company has adopted the Tata Business Excellence Model for managing the Company's business in an efficient and transparent manner. The Company has complied with the guidelines on Corporate Governance laid down by the Stock Exchanges.

The present Board comprises of 10 members being 2 Executive Directors (EDs) and 8 Non-Executive Directors (NEDs). Of the 8 NEDs, Four are Independent Directors, Two are Government Nominee Directors and other two represent the Promoters. The NEDs with their diverse knowledge, experience and expertise bring in their independent judgement in the deliberations and decisions of the Board. Apart from the sitting fees paid for attending Board/ Committee Meetings, the NEDs did not have any material pecuniary relationship or transactions with the Company, during the year 2001-02. The Company has a Non-Executive Chairman and the number of Independent Directors is more than one-third of the total number of Directors. The number of NEDs is more than 50 per cent of the total number of Directors. The Company, therefore, meets with the requirements relating to the composition of Board of Directors.

The Audit Committee has been functioning since July 2000. On 16th October, 2001, the Audit Committee was reconstituted and its terms of reference, role and scope were modified so as to bring them in line with Clause 49 of the Listing Agreement with the stock exchanges. The Company also complies with the provisions of the recently introduced Section 292A of the Companies Act, 1956, pertaining to the Audit Committee and its functioning. The scope of the Committee includes:

- Review of the Company's financial reporting process, the financial statements and financial/risk management policies.
- Review of the adequacy of the internal control systems in the Company.
- Review of the internal audit report forwarded by the internal auditors.
- Discussions with the management and the external auditors, the audit plan for the financial year and a joint post-audit review of the same.

During the year 2001, six Audit Committee meetings were held on 26th July, 20th August, 28th September and 29th October in 2001 and 22nd January and 6th March in 2002. The Audit Committee meetings are held both at Corporate Office and other locations and usually attended by the Finance Head and the representatives of internal auditors and statutory auditors are also invited. The Company Secretary acts as the Secretary to the Audit Committee. The then Chairman of the Audit Committee was also present at the last Annual General Meeting of the Company.

The Company is not having any Remuneration Committee as it felt not necessary to have such Committee. However, Remuneration Committee, if required, will be formed. At present, two Executive Directors have been appointed by the Company and whose terms and conditions of appointment and payment of remuneration have been fixed by the shareholders in the Extraordinary General Meeting held on 1st December. The Non-Executive Directors are entitled for sitting fee only for attending the Board/Committee meetings.

The aggregate value of salary and perquisites paid to Mr. P.K.De, former Director (Technical) and Dr. P. Dasgupta, former Director (Business Development), during the year 2001-02 was Rs. 12.13 lakhs and Rs. 6.41 lakhs respectively. The aggregate value of salary and perquisites paid to Mr. S.S.Ghosh, Managing Director and CEO and Mr. R.Ramanan, Dy. Managing Director and COO during the year 2001-02 was Rs. 14.44 lakhs and Rs. 3.20 lakhs respectively.

The Share Transfer Committee was constituted by the Board of Directors on 21st March, 1997 for consideration and approval of various requests for transfer, sub-division, consolidation, renewal, exchange, issue of new certificates in replacement of old certificates, as may be received from the Shareholders from time to time. On 29th October, 2001 Share Transfer Committee and the Shareholders/ Investors Grievance Committees were clubbed into one as 'Share Transfer-cum-Shareholders Grievance Committee'.

Mr. S. S. Ghosh, Managing Director and CEO, headed this Committee upto 14th May, 2002. However, as per requirement of the Corporate Governance norms, the Committee is now headed by a Non-Executive Independent Director Mr. Surendra Singh w.e.f. 14th May, 2002. The Committee has been formed to specially approve the share received for transfer and redressal of shareholders grievances. The Company Secretary attends the meeting and apprise the Committee of the nature of complaints received and dealt with and also the process for share transfers, etc.

Issues for Consideration

In view of the various conditions, the following issues are to be considered for effective corporate governance in the present scenario:

- Public awareness and educational efforts are needed to promote better understanding of essential corporate governance principles and their relationship to democratic development.
- Companies need to undertake voluntary reforms by developing codes of conduct and best practices guidelines.
- Independent, non-executive company directors with diverse talents and experience need to be appointed to corporate boards in larger numbers.
- The Boards must set goals for the CEOs and functional directors separately and collectively to measure their performance.
- The Board of Directors need to fulfill the following responsibilities:
  - Creating conditions for developing a sound business strategy in consonance with national plan objectives;

- Ensuring that the enterprise has a CEO of the highest caliber and grooming certain senior managers to assume the CEO's position in future;
- Creating systems of information, audit, and control to oversee whether the enterprise is meeting its objectives;
- Ensuring that the company complies with legal and ethical standards;
- Ensuring that the enterprise is well equipped in prevention and management of crisis;

■ All the organisations need to create confidence, trust and continued interest in the companies for future growth;

■ The gloval investors are to be attracted with the right leadership, responsiveness and effective governance.

6

Corporate Governance for Building Global Competence

Rajesh Sashittal

First of all, I would like to thank the School of Management Studies, Gayatri Vidya Parishad College for Degree and PG Courses for having invited me here to speak on this topic "Corporate Governance for Building Global Competence" a topic which touches us all in our everyday life, whether we are aware of it or not but touches us it does.

I am very happy that the School of Management Studies has chosen such an apt subject for this National Seminar. The realization that there still are institutions which give importance to and devote so much of their resources to a theme which had its origins may be more than ten years ago fills my heart with joy; for it is such institutions which redeem our faith in a system and form a firm foundation which enable us to keep our flag flying high.

The idea of corporate governance first took root as an economic principle when we first heard of it in the late 1990s, with the focus being maximization of profits so that the shareholders get their due. Several questions arose thereafter, leading to detailed studies made, the most notable being that of the Cadbury Committee, whose recommendations in the late 90's formed a sort of watershed in the issue of Corporate Governance. Among the many recommendations made by the committee, the most controversial and revolutionary requirement was that the "Directors should report on the effectiveness of a Company's system of internal control". This requirement meant that the internal controls extended beyond financial controls, sent shivers down many a corporate director's spine and this is what created the controversy. For hitherto financial controls had been very easily delegated and were the responsibility of the internal audit system.

This requirement was significantly watered down by the Paul Ruthman Committee, to restrict this clause to Internal Financial Control only.

Later committees extended some of the nuances of the Cadbury report to cover all relevant control objectives including financial, operational and compliance controls and business risk assessment and minimizing the risk of fraud.

One of the most common factors underlying past business failures was found to be the lack of an effective risk management mechanism. This was one area where, as I said earlier the challenge was being passed on to the internal audit function.

The shareholders were after all entitled to ask whether all significant risks were reviewed and why a particular wealth destroying event was not anticipated and acted upon.

The board of directors was therefore required to confirm that there was an on going process for identifying, evaluating and managing key business risks.

It is only fair that the shareholders should be aware of the risks that the corporates are taking and whether such risks have been properly evaluated or not.

From this subsequently evolved the Best Practices Code to be adopted by corporates to promote transparency and accountability in the actions of companies. Companies only stand to gain by adopting such systems and practices that promote transparency, accountability and fair dealings which bolster investor confidence.

I heard somewhere recently that several empirical studies proved that there was a very strong correlation between companies and markets which operated in an environment of strong corporate governance and higher returns in the long-run.

In India, the genesis of this idea of corporate governance coincided more or less with economic liberalization, privatization and globalization that started in the latter half of the 90's—a very happy coincidence indeed. For earlier, we operated in a highly protected environment, like the Russians and the Chinese behind their iron or bamboo curtains.

As we are all aware, the opening up of all the markets evinced a lot of interest amongst the international community in India. Coupled with this the East Asian crises gave us a good break, as the international community was looking for alternatives to invest their funds and India slowly started to emerge as that alternative with immense scope.

It is in this context that the concept of corporate governance is acquiring added significance. Capital, global or domestic will always find its own equilibrium and shall definitely flow to areas where it is well protected; it will definitely go past markets where there is limited or no protection. Companies that follow the Best Practices Code, shall therefore surely attract more capital as investors shall feel fully secure in the knowledge that their interests are well protected.

Hence the role of the regulators cannot be emphasized enough. In our corporate arena we have the Department of Company Affairs and for the stock markets, SEBI which are effective watchdogs for corporate India and of late SEBI has played its role admirably as recent events have shown.

The office of the independent director which is all set to become mandatory shortly is also a step in the right direction in promoting transparency, accountability and fairness, despite reservations in various quarters as to how independent is the independent director. What is important to note though is the fact that institutions promoting fairness and probity are gradually being strengthened.

The latest amongst various measures, though were applicable in the field of administration, is the Right to Information Act which became operative from October 2005; the Act as we all know, gives the individual powers to probe transactions of the administration.

In the area of banking also, we have the Reserve Bank of India which supervises the operations of the banks in India. The Governor of the Reserve Bank of India Dr. Y. V. Reddy announced in December last a gradual withdrawal from what was perceived as excessive controls by withdrawing their nominee directors from the boards of private sector Banks, although observers have been posted in certain cases where such Banks are yet to comply with the Reserve Bank of India guidelines on ownership of governance. It is felt that the need for such observers will decrease as the level of compliance increases.

In the case of public sector banks, the Government of India and the Reserve Bank of India still have their nominee directors. But the accent has been on moving away from external regulation to a regime of internal controls and regulation to promote transparency and fairness.

Thus the operation of the Best Practices Code, the office of the independent director and the Right to Information Act, should go a long way in increasing transparency, accountability and fairness in business dealings.

As I mentioned earlier, India is now a major destination for foreign investors, though we have miles to go before we catch up with China. Global investors are going to look for good practices, openness and transparency in dealings and strong indicators that their investments are well protected.

In this, the individual corporates themselves have a role, that of maintaining proper internal controls, financial, operational and controls relating to compliance and last but not the least, business risk assessment and minimizing the risk of fraud, which finds mention earlier. These are the basic indicators that foreign investors are going to look for, before investing their funds in India, these are the steps to be followed by Indian corporates if they wish to attract foreign capital.

There are of course, companies which do not wish to have direct foreign investments in their companies for fear of losing control of their empires. But on a broader canvas we can see the huge amounts invested by foreign institutional investors in our stock markets, which have kept the markets buoyant. It is imperative for even companies which do not wish to have direct foreign investments in their companies, to operate in a transparent mode with best practices, if they are to reap the benefits of such a buoyant market, for money will flow only to such good corporates and bypass those with a dubious record.

Corporate governance is an on going process of internal control and there is no quick fix solution or a one-size-fits-all design and each corporate and every industry has to keep reviewing its performance in the matter of such internal controls. There is a need to keep changing the requirements for maintaining internal controls to keep up pace with business which is always in a dynamic situation.

This is the reason, I said in the beginning, I was very happy that the School of Management at the Gayatri Vidya Parishad has chosen this theme for the National Seminar. As we all know, eternal vigilance is the price of liberty and it is heartening to note that even a decade after the seeds of corporate governance were sown, the subject still excites us and there are institutions, apart from corporates themselves which take so much interest in the running of business and commerce along ethical lines, with openness, transparency and fairness.

This augers very well for our country, which has already taken major steps into the international arena and is steadily making progress, an India which our young friends out there are going to take forward in the global field. Thanking you very much.

7

Corporate Governance: Concept and Practice (A Case Study of Infosys Ltd.)

P. Viswanadham, Mrs. Y. L. Lavanya and Mr. M. Vijay Kumar

Introduction

Corporate Governance in general is a mechanism to maximize the wealth of owners, which can be achieved by optimum utilization of resources and maximization of return in given economic environment by managing the organization in more transparent and participating ways. Corporate Governance has been seen by many as a combination of corporate ethics, corporate transparency, as well as corporate accountability.

Corporate Governance is strongly affected by the relationship among the participants in the governance system like individual shareholders, employees, suppliers etc. Though, the role and relationship among these participants are focused through law, regulation and voluntary adaptation in Corporate Governance mechanism play the most crucial role promoting and protecting the interest of shareholders and policy holders.

Corporate governance is the expression, which is not capable of being precisely defined. However, broadly speaking, corporate governance denotes direction and control of the affairs of a company. The role of corporate governance is to ensure that the directors of a company are subject to their duties, obligations and responsibilities, to act in the best interest of their company, to give direction and to remain accountable to their shareholders and other beneficiaries for their actions.

The objectives before a business are to create wealth for the society, maintain and preserve that wealth efficiently and to share the wealth with the shareholders. Corporate governance is the method by which the aforesaid objectives are achieved.

What is Corporate Governance?

Corporate governance is a process or a set of systems and processes to ensure that a complaint is managed to suit the best interest of all, this may include structures and organizational matters.

Cadbury Committee report says, "Corporate Governance is the system by which companies are directed and controlled. Boards of directors are responsible for the governance of their companies. The shareholders' role in governance is to appoint the directors and the auditors, and to satisfy themselves that an appropriate governance structure is in place. The responsibilities of the board include setting the company's strategic aims, providing the leadership to put them into effect, supervising the management of the business and reporting to shareholders on their stewardship. The board's actions are subject to laws, regulations and the shareholders approval at the general meetings."

Kumar Mangalam Committee report emphasizes that the fundamental objective of Corporate Governance is enhancement of shareholders' value keeping in view the other stakeholders. Since the prime objective of Corporate Governance is to enhance the wealth of the shareholders and interest of all stakeholders, good financial governance is the basis of sound Corporate Governance.

Corporate Governance according to L.V.V. Iyer is "a set of systems and processes which ensure that a company is managed to the best interests of all the stakeholders. The set systems that help the task of corporate governance should include certain structural and organizational aspects; the process that helps corporate governance will embrace how things are done within such structure and organizational systems."

Similar views also have been offered by Dr. Narang in his Development of Corporate Governance in India: "Corporate governance is a broad and somewhat vague term used to refer to a range of corporate controls and accountability mechanism designed to meet the aims of corporate stockholders. Corporate governance has also been defined to cover the concepts, theories and practices of board and its directors, and the relationships between board and the shareholders. Thus, corporate governance, as is generally understood, is the process of direction, supervision and accountability of corporations.

A minimal definition given by the CII Task Force, leads one to believe that whatever maximizes shareholder values must necessarily maximize corporate values. The definition reads: "Corporate governance deals with laws, procedures, practices and implicit rules that determine a company's ability to take managerial decision vis-à-vis its claimants-in particular, its shareholders, creditors, the State and employees. There is global consensus on the objective of 'good' corporate governance: Maximizing long-term shareholder value. Since shareholders are residual claimants, this objective follows from a premise that in well-performing capital and financial markets, whatever maximizes shareholder value must necessarily maximize corporate value, and best satisfy the claims of creditors, employees and the State."

The new corporate responsibilities have been well explained by Alvin Toffler in his The Third Wave (1980) To quote: "A corporation is no longer responsible simply for making a profit or producing goods but for simultaneously contributing to the solution to extremely complex ecological, moral, political, racial, sexual, and social problems. Instead of clinging to a sharply specialized economic function, the corporation prodded by criticism, legislation and its own concerned executives, is becoming a multipurpose institution." This definition recognizes the new awakening in the boardrooms regarding ecological and other trans-economic aspects of corporate actions. Various economic issues, thus, form part to corporate governance. Accordingly, the benefits of efficient performance should accrue to the shareholders, suppliers, consumers, employees, lenders, and indeed, to the society, in general.

Corporate Governance refers to the set of rules to the direction and control company (Cardon Report, Belgium). Corporate Governance describes the legal and factual Regulatory framework for managerial and supervising a company (Berlin Initiative Code, Preamble). Corporate Governance in the sense of the set of rules according to which firms are managed and controlled is the result of norms, traditional and pattern of behaviour developed by each economic and legal system (Preda Report, Italy).

Scope of the Corporate Governance

Corporate Governance mechanism is to be focused basically to protect the rights of shareholders and should ensure the equitable treatment of all shareholders. Corporate governance should encourage and ensure active co-operation between corporation and stakeholders to enhance the wealth, jobs and to sustain the financial health of the organization. Corporate Governance mechanism must promote a system of transparency and timely disclosure of information regarding performance, financial health, and ownership statistics and governance system of the organization. Corporate Governance mechanism must ensure independence of Board and its accountability to the company and stakeholders.

Good governance encompasses all aspects i.e.,—economic, political, administrative, social and judicial environment. Board must create balance of interest of capital providers with other stakeholders. Role of financial, non-financial, human and social capital must be recognized and create an environment for optimum utilization. Promote a culture innovation, creativity and entrepreneurship in the organization. Put in place a more dynamic non-partisan Board with executive and non-executive directors of repute and accountability. Strengthen the Board of Directors maintain independence of nominee directors. Promoter's ethical practices of the board since they are engine of growth. Concern about people, their rile, innovation and efficiency, improvement and to create an environment of self-actualization. Foster creativity-transparency and build trust in Organization.

Corporate Governance Models

Though the objectives are same in all the countries as a mechanism to strengthen corporate accountability in order to enhance shareholders wealth, the approach and instruments are quite different to the USA—the country with maximum social respect and responsibilities for corporate, has adopted a soft approach towards corporate governance to minimize the conflict between owners and manager by giving financial incentive (stock options). Stock exchanges (through listing conditions) play an important role in imparting transparency and accountability of the corporate managers. Towards installing transparency in corporate activities, inside trading has been made illegal and disclosure norms are also made an essential part of corporate governance in USA.

The unique characteristics and distinctive features of four important models of corporate governance models are discussed:

The German Model

The system of corporate governance in Germany is much less driven by the stock market than that in the USA but implemented through interaction and consensus of Management Board and Supervisory Board. In Germany, banks play an important role in the market because of its role as holders of company's stocks and providers of long-term finance. 'Supervisory' and 'Management Boards' run the banks. While the Supervisory Board is responsible for the "company's accounts, major capital expenditures, strategic acquisition and closures, dividends and most importantly for appointment to the Management Board, the Management Board is responsible for running the company." The two-tier Board structure in Germany institutionalizes some checks and balances. Unlike in the USA, where banks cannot trade in securities, banks in Germany not only provide long-term finance but also hold stocks of companies. Banks also have positions on the top tier of the two-tiered board system.

Although both the USA and Germany represent market-based systems and compete aggressively across the globe Germany's system of corporate governance is reflected in the absolute power given to a president director-general in each company and this position is considered stronger than that of the CEO in the US.

The German Model

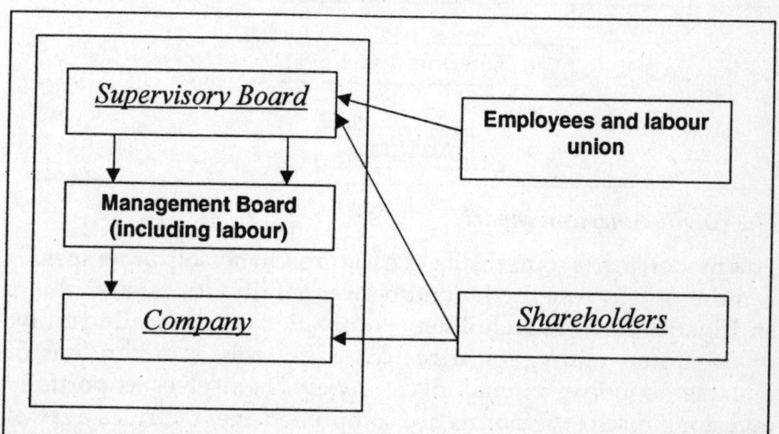

The Japanese Model

However, in Japan the basic approach has been developed on an obligation to company, country and family which is implemented through cross holding and networking among group companies. Thus the focus on the board is less significant in Japan. Japanese corporate are more concerned about appreciation of the value of yen, promotion of entrepreneurial and innovative talents of its people for the development of society and how best to hold them accountable. The Ministry of International Trade and Industry and Ministry of Finance provide them with useful information and impetus for strategizing their operations in world markets.

The Japanese Model

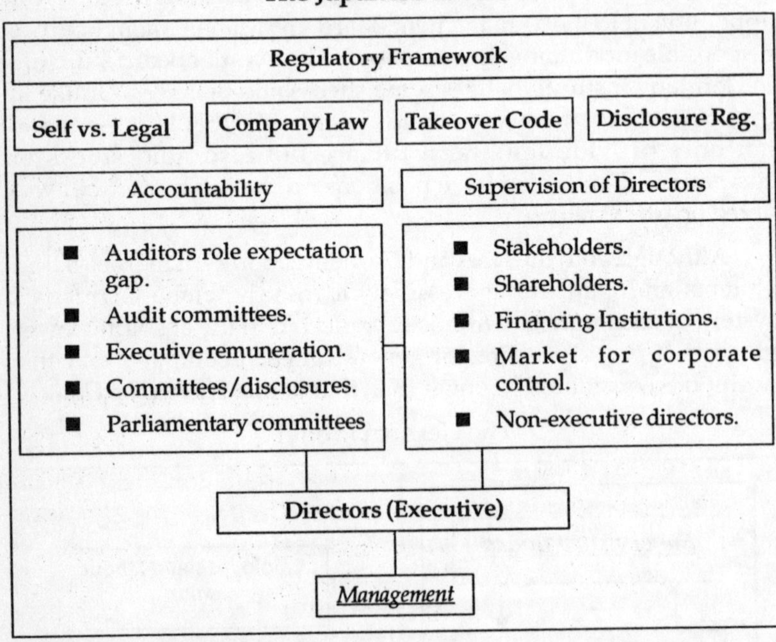

The Anglo-American Model

This model carries some distinctive feature: Ownership of companies is more or less equally divided between individual shareholders and institutional shareholders; companies are typically run by professional managers; directors are rarely independent of management; institutional investor view themselves as portfolio investors; disclosure norms are comprehensive; the rules against insider trading and penalties for price manipulations are stiff, and there is fairly active market for corporate control that provides a credible threat of takeover to constant under-performers. The Anglo-American model, as characterized by Jonathan Charkham, is a 'high-tensions model' because of the important role of the CEO, active capital markets, short-termism and credible takeover threats.

The Anglo-American Model

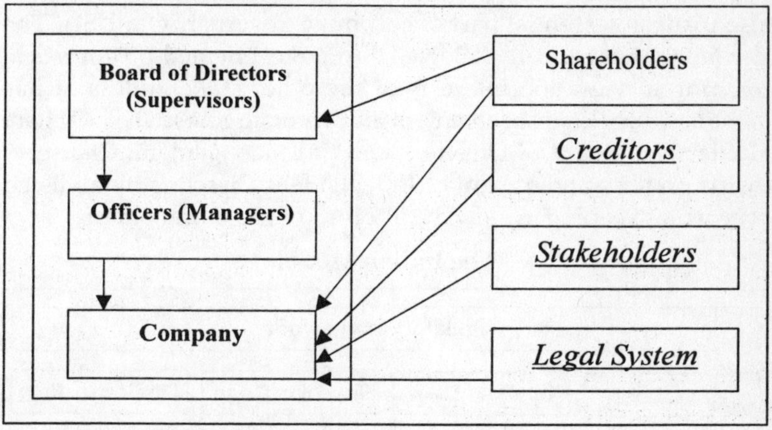

Corporate Governance Model in India

Corporate Governance is the current buzzword in India as well as the world over. The concept of Corporate Governance became popular after 1990s, though few Corporate have been practicing in earlier. The new paradigm of corporate governance is in tune with the changing times, in keeping with the demand for greater accountability of companies to shareholders and customers, economic liberalization and deregulation of industry and business, and other factors. The Cadbury Committee Report has also given fillip to the debate on corporate governance in India.

The SEBI Committee popularly known as Kumar Mangalam Committee, on corporate governance had submitted its final report on February 2000. The Committee has reviewed the fundamental objective of corporate governance as enhancement of shareholders' value. A concerted effort is being made now and a structured approach is being evolved with the recommendations of Kumar Mangalam Committee Report. The Committee has basically followed the market oriented US approach – The USA – the country with maximum social respect and responsibilities for corporate, has adopted a soft approach towards corporate governance to minimize the conflict between owners and manager by giving financial incentive (stock options), stock exchanges (through listing conditions) play an important role in imparting transparency and accountability of the Corporate Managers. Accountability of the Corporate Managers. Towards instilling transparency in corporate activities, inside trading has been made illegal and disclosure norms also made an essential part of corporate governance in USA. The Committee has basically followed the market oriented US approach. Keeping in view the interests of the other stakeholders, it has identified three key constituents of the corporate governance: *(i)* Share Holders; *(ii)* Board of Directors and *(iii)* Management. Clause 49 insists on the appointment of Independent Directors by all listed companies keeping in view the interests of the shareholders.

The Indian Model

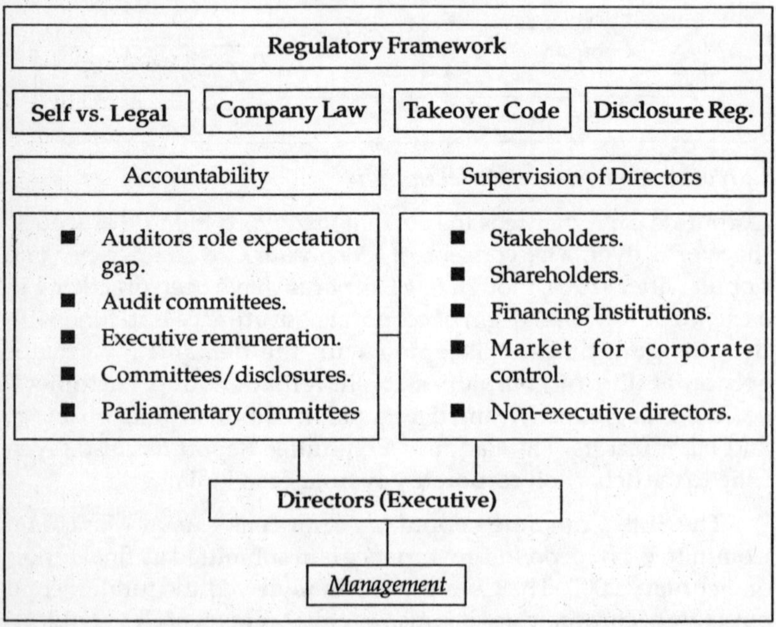

Instruments of Governance

Regulatory mechanism set the basic framework of Corporate Governance but it is the commitment and involvement of management, which can translate the objective into practice. The practice of Corporate Governance can be strengthening through guidance of Board and other committees like Audit Committee, Investment Committee. While the Board and committees should take keen interest in corporate practices and governance, management should also support them by providing regular information.

(i) *Board:* The Board of the Company plays the most crucial role in translating the Corporate Governance practices into reality by setting goals and guiding corporate strategy, monitoring performance, potential conflicts, providing suggestions to mitigate them and by ensuring effectiveness of Governance practices. However, effectiveness of the Board Governance also depends on the composition and independence of Board. In an Insurance Company a wide range of activities are performed which require close monitoring of the Board, but the Board should specially keep a close watch on the following and the management should periodically submit its report to the Board on the following; Capital Adequacy, Solvency Margin, Developments in Capital Market, Interest Rate Scenario and Sensitivity Analysis, Investment Strategy, Regulatory Compliance Periodic Disclosure etc.

(ii) *Audit Committee:* Audit Committee has been described as the watchdog of the Corporate Governance System. "The Audit Committee acts as the bridge between the Board of the Statutory Auditors and Internal Auditors." The Audit Committee performs a wide range of functions related to the financial management of the company – overseeing financial reporting, process of disclosure, accounting policies and practices. In each of the meeting of the Audit Committee the following items should be placed before it. Financial Results of the Company, Review of Findings of Internal Auditors, Control System and Lapses in System and Procedure, Risk Management Policy.

(iii) *Investment Committee:* Investment Management is the most crucial function of an insurance company, since it deals with long-term liability and invests in uncertain capital market full of various types of risks as mentioned above. Investment Management, therefore need to take into account of these

uncertainties and risks under a well-governed system and practices. Investment Committee should guide to frame Investment Policy, Investment Strategy; Portfolios risk Management Strategy, Turnover Strategy etc. Investment Committee should be supplied the following information—Capital Market Development, Interest rate scenario, changes in Investment Strategy, changes in Portfolio, Turnover Statistics, and Health of Portfolio including NPA, Investment Performance and Income.

(iv) *Prudent Person Rules:* Efficiency Management of Insurance Company significantly influenced by accounting and actuarial functions calls for efficiency in Management of funds, accounting and valuation of assets and pricing of products, provisioning for liabilities etc., as per the quantitative and qualitative guidelines fixed by the regulators. However, quantitative regulations have a limit to monitor the operation and potential solvency. Quantitative Regulations, therefore, need to be supplemented by the Prudent Person Rules and internal ethical standard and Governance System set up by the insurers. These together will contribute to the operational transparency and disclosure. However, the insurer, in line with Regulator, must set up the norms for operational transparency and standard of disclosure, which would enhance the involvement of stakeholders in the organization.

Corporate Governance—A Case Study of Infosys Ltd.

Infosys was incorporated in the state of Maharastra, in India on July 1981. It ranked No.1 employer in the IT sector. Company is best employer in India. Infosys gets best annual report awards of the Chartered Accountants of India for seventh successive year. It ranked the most globally competitive and best managed company. The company has a written disclosure policy, which coverts interacting with all external constituents such as analyst, fund managers and the media.

Corporate Governance Practices of Infosys

Infosys corporate governance philosophy is based on the following principles.

- Satisfy the spirit of the law and not just the letter of the law but it is beyond the law.
- Be transparent and maintain high degree of disclosers level. When in doubt disclose.
- Make a clear distinction between personal conveniences and corporate resources.
- Communicate externally, in a truthful manner, about how they run company internally.
- Comply with the law in all countries in which they operate.
- Have a simple and transparent corporate structure driven solely by the business needs.
- Management is the trustee of the shareholders capital and not the owner.

The disclosures of corporate governance in Infosys covered the following areas:

(a) Board Composition

1. Size and composition of the board.
2. Responsibilities of the chairman, CEO and COO.
3. Board definition of independent directors.
4. Board membership criteria.
5. Selection of new directors.
6. Membership criteria.
7. Retirement Policy.
8. Succession Planning.
9. Board Compensation Review.
10. Membership of the boards.

(b) Board Meetings

1. Scheduling and selection of agenda items for board meetings.
2. Availability of information to the members of the board.
3. Independent directors discussion.
4. Materially significant related party transactions.

(c) *Board Committees*

Currently, the board has six committees—the audit committee, the compensation committee, the nomination committee, the investors grievance committee, the investment committee and the share transfer committee. The first three consist entirely of independent directors. The investors grievance committee is composed of an independent, non-executive chairman and some executive and non-executive directors. The investment committee and the share transfer committee consist of all executive directors.

The board is responsible for the consulting, assigning, co-opting and fixing of terms of service for committee members to various committees, and it delegates these powers to the nominations committee.

The chairman of the board, in consultation with the company secretary of the company and the committee chairman, determines the frequency and duration of the committee meetings. Normally, all the committees and the share transfer committees, which meet as and when the need arises. Typically the meetings of the audit, compensation and nominations committees last for the better part of a working day. Recommendations of the committee are submitted to the full board for approval. The quorum for meetings is that either two members or one-third of the members of the committees, whichever is higher.

1. *Audit Committee*

In India, Infosys is listed on the Stock Exchange, Mumbai (or the BSE), the National Stock Exchange(NSE) and the Bangalore Stock Exchange(BSE). In the US, it is listed on the NASDAQ. In India, Clause 49 of the Listing Agreement makes it mandatory for listed companies to adopt an, appropriate audit committee charter. The Blue Ribbon Committee set up by the US Securities and Exchange Commission (SEC) recommended that every listed company adopt and audit committee charter, which has been adopted by NASDAQ.

In it's meeting on May 27, 2000, Infosys' audit committee adopted a charter, which meets the requirement of Clause 49 of the Listing Agreement with Indian stock exchange and the SEC. It is given below. The audit committee of Infosys comprises six independent directors.

1.1 *Audit Committee Charter*
It includes followings:

- Primary objectives of the audit committee
- Responsibilities of the audit committee
- Compensation of the audit committee
- Relationship with independent and internal auditors
- Disclosure requirement
- Meetings and reports
- Delegation of authority
- Definition

1.2 *Details of audit committee attendance*

1.3 *Audit committee report*

2. *Compensation Committee*

2.1 *Compensation committee charter*
Which includes followings:

- Purpose
- Committee membership and organization
- Committee responsibility and authority

2.2 *Compensation committee-attendance*

2.3 *Compensation committee reports*

3. *Nomination Committee*

3.1 *Nomination committee charter*

- Purpose
- Committee membership and organization
- Committee responsibilities and authority

3.2 *Nomination committee attendance*

3.3 *Nomination committee reports*

5. *Investment Committee*
   - Reports of Investment Committee
6. *Share Transfer Committee*

(d) ***Management Review and Responsibility***

1. Formal evalution of officers
2. Board interaction with clients, employees, institutional investors, the government and the press
3. Risk Management
4. Management discussion and analysis

(e) ***Shareholders***

1. Disclosures regarding appointment or re-appointment of directors
2. Communication to share holders
3. Investors grievances and share transfer
4. Details of non-compliance
5. General body meetings
6. Postal ballots
7. Auditors certificate on corporate governance

(f) ***Compliance with the recommendations of the report of the committee on corporate audit and governance (Naresh Chandra Committee)***

(g) ***Compliance with international corporate Governance-2000 guidelines.***

1. Euro share holders corporate Governance guidelines-2000.
2. Compliance with findings and recommendations of the Conference Board, Commission on Public Trust and Private Enterprises in the US.
3. Corporate Governance report as per guidelines of:
   - The Australian Stock Exchange.
   - Committee of Canadian Institute of Chartered Accountants.

- The Higgs and Smith reports
- Finance Commission reports
- Germany Commission reports
- Japan Commission reports.

Infosys is Investor's friendly company committed to the highest standard of the disclosers. It also voluntarily provide unaudited financial statements prepare in substantial complies with the GAAP requirement Australia, Canada, France, Germany, Japan, United Kingdom, US. and India. It provides statement on complies with these standards in the respective national language of these countries.

Conclusion

Corporate governance provides broad partners of accountability, control and reporting system by the Board as it encompasses the interactive relationship among various constituents in determining directions and performances of business organizations. The issues and the challenges before the business community have never been as turbulent and unpredictable as they are today, following the globalization of business. Intensive competition, emerging new multilateral trading order and the need for sustainable development have generated extensive debate on the process and style of Corporate Governance.

REFERENCES

1. *Corporate Governance, What it means and what it needs,* Management Review, July-December, 1996.
2. *C.G. World Wide,* Management Review, July-December, 1996.
3. *Corporate Governance: What needs to be done,* Fortune India, January 16-31, 1997.
4. *Corporate Governance, Multi faceted issue,* Chartered Secretary, May 1997.
5. *Proceedings of Silver Jubilee National Convention of ICSI,* Chartered Secretary, October, 1997.
6. *Corporate Governance, Time for a Metamorphosis, The Hindu,* July 9, 1997.
7. *Business Today,* May, 7-21, 1997.
8. N. Gopalaswamy, *Corporate Governance—The New Paradigm,* Wheeler Publishing, A Division of A.H. Wheeler and Co., Ltd., New Delhi, 1998.
9. Indian Banks Association, Indian Banking Book, Mumbai, 2003.
10. Vepakesam, "Corporate Governance", Reserve Bank of India Bulletin, January 2000, pp. 21-43.

8

Corporate Governance in Banking Sector

A. U. Durga Devi and P.M. Soundharyam

The Banking Sector plays a crucial role in the economic development of a nation. An efficient, effective, vibrant and innovative banking Stimulates economic growth by mobilizing earnings and by efficiently allocating funds for productive purposes. Indian Banking industry underwent repeated restructuring and revitalizing since rationalization.

On a recent survey entitled Banking Institutions in Developing Markets, the World Bank comments, "Banking is in the midst of change. As Governments seek to improve economic efficiency and better allocation of natural resources. Policy makers are shifting economics towards openness, competition and market discipline. Privatization is spreading and state firms, including banks that were once highly regulated, are being given greater autonomy to survive and prosper, bankers must jettison their bureaucratic culture and become competitive entrepreneurs, responding and adapting to market economy."

Corporate Governance reiterates the role of managers in the corporate world. When the ownership and management differ as in the case of companies, the executives owe responsibility to all the stakeholders and all others whom they deal with on how the company is managed. It tries to enunciate the responsibility of Board of Directors and Managers, whether defined by the law or not, to ensure good performance.

Corporate Governance establishes the relationship between the shareholders and other stakeholders with the management and its Board.

The principles of Corporate Governance should contribute to make every company a responsible corporate citizen. A responsible corporate citizen should not only enhance the shareholders' wealth but also exhibit fairness to other stakeholders like consumers, employees and the community in general. Maximization of shareholders' wealth has to be achieved adherence to ethical values and transparency in dealings.

The demand to make the Board of directors and Management accountable and the need for ethical practices in corporate management and adherence to the law of the were responsible for the emergence of Corporate Governance.

The Basel Committee published its paper on "Enhancing Corporate Governance for Banking organizations" in September 1999.

Basel issued this paper to supervisory authorities worldwide to assist them in promoting the adoption of sound Corporate Governance practices in banking organizations. The Basel Committee recognizes that Corporate Governance is much broader in case of Banks. Banks are critical components of an economy and cater to a large segment of the population in a country. Hence banks should have strong Corporate Governance, though banking is regulated industry.

Corporate Governance principles in India are still in an evolutionary stage. Governance does not mean replicating or following codes prevalent worldwide. The strongest impetus for change must come from the Directors and the Management themselves. Thanks to new policy initiatives and thrusts, the Indian Corporate landscape has undergone tremendous metamorphosis, bringing in its wake new challenges and problems. Corporate governance, against this backdrop, requires taking some bold initiatives.

Corporate Governance in a service industry like banks is not only to ensure compliance with regulatory requirements but also to be responsive to the expectations of all the stakeholders who deal with the Banks. Banks shall strive for excellence with the twin objectives of enhancing customer satisfaction and shareholder value. The Board of Directors shall support the broad principles of Corporate Governance.

The functioning of Boards of public sector banks is still regulated, as the Nationalised Banks (Management) Scheme is yet to be amended in line with the current trends. However, operational flexibility is given in several areas, which will facilitate adopting Corporate Governance in banks.

Reserve Bank of India has initiated various measures to improve Corporate Governance in the Indian banks. Arising out of Basel Committee recommendations, the Reserve Bank of India introduced Capital Adequacy measures for Indian banks. The ratio of capital to risk adjusted assets is being progressively increased, to fall in line with the international standards. For the year ending 31st March 2002, Banks are required to maintain a minimum CAR of 9 per cent. Banks are increasingly relying on the capital requirements. To pave way for the Public Sector Banks (PSBs) to access the capital market, the Nationalization Act was amended in the year 1994. As the ownership of the PSBs gets broad, individual shareholders and institutional shareholders would find more importance. The secondary market price of shares will depend on the quality of governance, vision of the Board, its ability to face and preempt crises and key performance indicators such as Earnings Per Share (EPS), Return On Assets (ROA), Return On Equity (ROE) and Economic Value Added (EVA).

Banks are required to maintain a minimum CAR of 9 per cent. Banks are increasingly relying on the Capital requirements. To pave the way for the Public Sector Banks (PSBs) to access the capital market, the Nationalization Act was amended in the year 1994. As the ownership of the PSBs gets broad, individual shareholders and institutional shareholders would find more importance.

Features of Good Corporate Governance Principles

- Openness, integrity and accountability must be the key elements of Corporate Governance.
- Functioning of the Boards needs to undergo a qualitative change if they are to meet the expectations of external constituencies.
- A bifurcation of the role of the Chairman and the Managing Director may ensure that Chairman is free from operational chores and is able to give focused attention to the working of the Board.

- Composition of the Board shall be broad based through the induction of independent Directors and the Board should adopt Code of Corporate Governance. Recently, a few public sector banks including Corporation Bank, inducted shareholders representatives on their Boards.
- Code of best practices shall be evolved to achieve the necessary high standards of corporate behaviour.

The emergence of capital adequacy, income recognition, asset classification norms, the requirements of improved disclosure and transparency have enhanced dependability of the financial statements in respect of banking companies.

Falling in line with SEBI directives, the listed banking companies have started disclosing their performance on quarterly basis. Unlisted banks are yet to do this. Banks have even resorted to Analysts/ investors meet at periodical intervals to update their investors. Though theses are positive indications, still lot more is required to be done.

The emergence of capital adequacy, income recognition, asset classification norms, the requirements of improved disclosure and transparency have enhanced dependability of the financial statements in respect of banking companies.

Some Suggestions

- Eminent men who can contribute towards the vision, control and guidance of banks should be chosen as Directors.
- Bifurcation of the post of the Chairman and Managing Director, so that Chairman is free operational chores and is able to give focused attention to the working of the Board.
- Boards should have a formal schedule of matters reserved for them for decision to ensure that the direction and control of the Bank is firmly in their hands.
- Non-executive directors should be conversant with the bank's accounts. Their calibre should be such that their views carry significant weight in the Board's decisions.
- Re-appointment of non-executive directors should be based on appraisal of their contribution to the board's functioning. Directors who have not been present for at least 50 per cent

of the board meeting should not be considered for reappointment.

- Chairman and Managing Director should have a minimum tenure of two years to ensure proper direction and continuity of policy.
- The Board shall form an effective audit committee comprising at least three non-executive directors and this committee should be given access to all financial information.
- The Report of the Board of Directors should contain information on monthly average share prices, performance of the Bank's share vis-à-vis the accepted stock price indices, shareholding pattern, credit defaults and provisions made thereof.
- The quality of shareholder communications should be improved. In addition to the annual reports, quarterly operational performance should also reach shareholders.
- The adoption of such a code of self-discipline for good governance will be a major step in self-regulation through concerted action by the Board Members and external auditors to improve the quality of governance in banks.

In the years to come, the Indian financial system will grow not only in size but also complexity as the forces of competition gain further momentum and as the financial markets acquire further expertise. The thrust to the second phase of reform would have to be on improvement in the organizational effectiveness of the corporate entities, banks and other financial institutions. It is in this context, the role of Corporate Governance assumes importance.

9

Corporate Governance—Its Implications in Banking Sector

Dr. S. S. Prasada Rao, G. V. S. Sekhar and S. Sheik

Any corporate entity whether it may public or private sector should need to make self-examination of their governance in the competitive world. Technological revolution has brought consistent changes in the pattern of corporate governance. It has reached centre-stage in the global agenda. The principles and codes evolved in several countries have furthered the cause of efficiency, transparency and equity particularly in the interest of the shareholders. Sustainable shareholder value has become the mantra for corporate immortality translating eventually into welfare of the society. The Standing Conference of Public Enterprises (SCOPE), New Delhi, had recognized in 1996, the need to examine the corporate governance issues relevant to the public sector undertakings in India i.e. those companies in which Central Government has equity of 51 per cent and above. The term "Public Enterprise" here has the broad international meaning covering various types of state owned/controlled enterprise.

The listed and the unlisted government companies, the central and the state level corporations, public sector banks, insurance and FIs, co-operatives and department undertakings are included in this term. The principles, if accepted, will obviously imply several operational difficulties, pulls, pressures and dilemmas. However, the attempt is to identify and gain consensus on the pillars for good corporate governance without being daunted by the potential controversies or operational barriers.

The Standing Conference of Public Enterprises (SCOPE), New Delhi, had recognised in 1996, the need to examine the corporate governance issues relevant to the public sector undertakings in India i.e. those companies in which Central Government has equity of 51 per cent and above. It was recognised that the codes, which were referred to (Cadbury's and the Confederation of Indian Industry's at that time), were most appropriate to the private sector and that the infirmities in the public enterprise governance needed a devoted attention. An attempt was made to address the special conditions of the central public sector undertakings, which are also publicly listed and traded on the stock exchanges, and Yaga Consulting prepared a report titled "Corporate Governance and the Public Sector Undertaking" in October, 1997.

Good corporate governance in public enterprises implies attention to issues larger than those of law and stock exchanges. They need to address the principles of government and public enterprise relationship and create the fundamental pillars based on which the governing board can become effective. The principles, codes and best practices for boards will become far more attractive and effective once these fundamentals are agreed upon and instituted.

Policy Implications in Corporate Governance

This paper has argued that the special nature of banking institutions necessitates a broad view of corporate governance where regulation of banking activities is required to protect depositors. In developed economies, protection of depositors in a deregulated environment is typically provided by a system of prudential regulation, but in developing economies such protection is undermined by the lack of well-trained supervisors, inadequate disclosure requirements, the cost of raising bank capital and the presence of distributional cartels. In order to deal with these problems, we suggest that developing economies need to adopt the following measures. Firstly, liberalisation policies need to be gradual, and should be dependent upon improvements in prudential regulation. Secondly, developing economies need to expend resources enhancing the quality of their financial reporting systems, as well as the quantity and quality of bank supervisors. Thirdly, given that bank capital plays such an important role in prudential regulatory systems, it may be necessary to improve investor protection laws, increase financial disclosure and impose fiduciary duties upon bank directos so that banks can raise the equity capital required for regulatory purposes. A further reason as to why this policy needs implemented is the growing recognition that the corporate governance of banks has an important role to play in assisting supervisory institutions to perform their tasks, allowing supervisors to have a working relationship with bank management, rather than adversarial one (BCBS, 1999). We have suggested that the corporate governance of banks in developing economies is severely affected by political considerations. Firstly, given the trend towards privatisation of government-owned banks in developing economies, there is a need for the managers of such banks to be granted autonomy and be gradually introduced to the corporate governance practices of the private sector prior to divestment. Secondly, where there has only been partial divestment and governments have not relinquished any control to other shareholders, it may prove very difficult to divest further ownership stakes unless corporate governance is strengthened. Finally, given that limited entry of foreign banks may lead to increased competition, which in turn encourages domestic banks to emulate the corporate governance practices of their foreign competitors, we suggest that developing economies partially open up their banking sector to foreign banks.

The framework for the principles of corporate governance has emanated from such a "world-view" and with the objective of creating efficient and transparent markets with widely held private ownership. Understandably, codes and principles in different countries have tended to believe that all enterprises will be of one variety only despite the caution that "one size doesn't fit all". Thus, public enterprises have been treated in the same manner as the private either with the assumption that what is good for one is good for the other, or on the premise that eventually all enterprises should be free of dominant ownership of the government.

Are Rules Chandged ?

The rules of corporate governance have changed in the present corporate form of administration. And there has been a range of reactions to this change. One can make a convincing case that companies maximize national well-being when they are focused doing what they do bet: running a profitable business within the limits of law and decency. In the domestic context, debates about corporate social responsibility have focused on whether a firm should adopt non-economic goals. We cannot find suitable answers to most troubling questions like: is the social responsibility of companies limited to making money for their shareholders? Or do they have larger role to play? In the age of globalization, corporations and business enterprises are no longer confined to the traditional boundaries of the nation-state. In the last 20 years, MNCs have played a key role in defining markets and influencing the behaviour of a large number of consumers. Those who argue for a narrow view of Corporate governance believe that a firm's only responsibility is to maximize the shareholders wealth within the law. Proponents of a broader view of this concept argue that firms should adopt the role of a good citizen and balance the interests of shareholders with the best interests of the society. Some opponents suspect the corporate team of cheating on their environments, both ecological and social, while others object fundamentally to the idea that a free market economy is beneficial to society.

When business goes global, across national and cultural borders the debate about CG takes on added layers of complexity. In particular, perplexing questions about the existence of universal ethical standards are raised. This is especially problematic when multinationals operate in host countries with different standards of business practice. The question of ethical relativity and CG arise not only in the context of different home and host country employment practices but also in the central operations and policies of multinationals. In this context, this paper focuses on three emerging perspectives that inform CG along with the survey results, and also analyzes international and Indian dimensions of people's ideas.

Corporate Governance in Banking Sector

The Reserve Bank of India (RBI) has asked all listed commercial banks to follow SEBI's committee report on corporate governance. Some of the important recommendations of the SEBI committee on corporate governance that will henceforth be applicable to listed commercial banks include, that all pecuniary relationship or transactions of the non-executive directors should be disclosed in the annual report. The committee has suggested that emphasis must be laid on the caliber of the non-executive directors, especially independent directors, since non-executive directors help bring an independent judgment to bear on the boards deliberations, especially on issues of strategy, performance, management of conflicts and standards of conduct. It has been recommended that the board of the company have an optimum combination of executive and non-executive directors with not less than 50 per cent of the board comprising the non-executive directors. The number of independent directors depends on the nature of the chairman of the board. In case a company has a non-executive chairman, at least half of the board should be independent (mandatory recommendation). According to the RBI circular, the audit committee of the board may look into the reasons for default in payment to depositors, debenture holders, shareholders (non-payment of dividends) and creditors, wherever there are any cases of defaults in payment.

Corporate Governance and the Special Nature of Banking

The narrow approach to corporate governance views the subject as the mechanism through which shareholders are assured that managers will act in their interests. Indeed, as far back as Adam Smith, it has been recognised that managers do not always act in the best interests of shareholders (Henderson, 1986). This problem has been especially exacerbated in the Anglo-Saxon economies by the evolution of the modern firm characterised by a large number of atomised shareholders, leading to a separation of ownership and control. (1) The separation of ownership and control has given rise to an agency problem whereby management operate the firm in their own interests, not those of shareholders (Jensen and Meckling, 1976; Fama and Jensen, 1983). This creates opportunities for managerial shirking or empire building and, in the extreme, outright expropriation. (2) However, there is a broader view of corporate governance, which views the subject as the methods by which suppliers of finance control managers in order to ensure that their capital cannot be expropriated and that they earn a return on their investment (Shleifer and Vishny, 1997, p. 737; Vives, 2000, p. 1; Oman, 2001, p.13).

We will argue below that the special nature of banking means that it is more appropriate to adopt the broader view of corporate governance for banks. Notably, Macey and O'Hara (2001) argue that a broader view of corporate governance should be adopted in the case of banking institutions, arguing that because of the peculiar contractual form of banking, corporate governance mechanisms for banks should encapsulate depositors as well as shareholders. As we shall see below, the special nature of banking requires not only a broader view of corporate governance, but also government intervention in order to restrain the behaviour of bank management.

Depositors do not know the true value of a bank's loan portfolio as such information is incommunicable and very costly to reveal, implying that a bank's loan portfolio is highly fungible (Bhattacharya *et. al.*, 1998, p. 761).

As a consequence of this asymmetric information problem, bank managers have an incentive each period to invest in riskier assets than they promised they would ex ante. In order to credibly commit that they will not expropriate depositors, banks could make investments in brand-name or reputational capital (Klein, 1974; Gorton 1994; Demetz *et. al.*, 1996; Bhattacharya *et. al.*, 1998), but these schemes give depositors little confidence, especially when contracts have a finite nature and discount rates are sufficiently high (Hickson and Turner, 2003). The opaqueness of banks also makes it very costly for depositors to constrain managerial discretion through debt covenants (Capiro and Levine, 2002, p. 2). Consequently, rational depositors will require some form of guarantee before they would deposit with a bank. Government-provided guarantees in the form of implicit and explicit deposit insurance might encourage economic agents to deposit their wealth with a bank, as a substantial part of the moral hazard cost is borne by the government. Nevertheless, even if the government provides deposit insurance, bank managers still have an incentive to opportunistically increase their risk taking, but now it is mainly at the government's expense. This well-known moral hazard problem can be ameliorated through the use of economic regulations such as asset restrictions, interest rate ceilings, separation of commercial banking from insurance and investment banking, and reserve requirements. Amongst the effects of these regulations is that they limit the ability of bank managers to over-issue liabilities or divert assets into high risk ventures. Thus far we have argued that the special nature of the banking firm requires public protection of depositors from opportunistic bank management. However, the special nature of the banking firm also affects the relationship between shareholders and managers. For example, the opaqueness of bank assets makes it very costly for diffuse equity holders to write and enforce effective incentive contracts or to use their voting rights as a vehicle for influencing firm decisions. Furthermore, the existence of deposit insurance may reduce the need for banks to raise capital from large, uninsured investors who have the incentive to exert corporate control (Capiro and Levine, 2002). A further issue is that the interests of bank shareholders may oppose those of governmental regulators, who have their own agendas, which may not necessarily coincide with maximising bank value. Shareholders may want managers to take more risk than is socially optimal, whereas regulators have a preference for managers to take substantially less risk due to their concerns about system-wide financial stability. Shareholders could motivate such risk-taking using incentive-compatible compensation schemes. However, from the regulators point of view, managers' compensation schemes should be structured so as to discourage banks from becoming too risky. For example, regulators could, through directives or moral suasion, restrict the issue of option grants to bank managers. Alternatively, regulators could vary capital requirements depending on the extent to which compensation policies encourage risk taking (Caprio and Levine, 2002, p. 22). Some economists argue that competition in the product or service market may act as a substitute for corporate governance mechanisms (Allen and Gale, 2000). The basic argument is that firms with inferior and expropriating management will be forced out of the market by firms possessing non-expropriating managers due to sheer competitive pressure. However the banking industry, possibly due to its information-intensive nature, may be a lot less competitive than other business sectors (Caprio and Levine, 2002). Therefore, this lack of competitive pressure as well as the special nature of banking suggests that banks may need stronger corporate governance mechanisms than other firms.

Deregulation of Banks in Developing Economies

In the above section we argued that the special nature of banking might require government-provided deposit insurance in order to protect depositors. Concomitantly, in order to ameliorate the associated moral hazard problem, we suggested that banks might need regulated. However, over the last two decades or so, many governments around the world have moved away from using these economic regulations towards using prudential regulation as part of their reform process in the financial sector. Prudential regulation involves banks having to hold capital proportional to their risk-taking, early warning systems, bank resolution schemes and banks being examined on an on-site and off-site basis by banking supervisors. The main objective of prudential regulation is to safeguard the stability of the financial system and to protect deposits. However, the prudential reforms already implemented in developing countries have not been effective in preventing banking crises, and a question remains as to how prudential systems can be strengthened to make them more effective (Brownbridge, 2002). The ability of developing economies to strengthen their prudential supervision is questionable for several reasons. Firstly, it is accepted that banks in developing economies should have substantially higher capital requirements than banks in developed economies. However, many banks in developing economies find it very costly to raise even small amounts of capital. Secondly, there are not enough well trained supervisors in developing economies to examine banks. Thirdly, supervisory bodies in developing economies typically lack political independence, which may undermine their ability to coerce banks to comply with prudential requirements and impose suitable penalties. Fourthly, prudential supervision completely relies on accurate and timely accounting information. However, in many developing economies, accounting rules, if they exist at all, are flexible, and typically, there is a paucity of information disclosure requirements. Therefore, if a developing economy liberalises without sufficiently strengthening it prudential supervisory system, bank managers will find it easier to expropriate depositors and deposit insurance providers. A prudential approach to regulation will typically result in banks in developing economies having to raise equity in order to comply with capital adequacy norms. Consequently, prior to developing economies deregulating their banking systems, much attention will need to be paid to the speedy implementation of robust corporate governance mechanisms in order to protect shareholders. However, in developing economies, the introduction of sound corporate governance principles into banking has been partially hampered by poor legal protection, weak information disclosure requirements and dominant owners (Arun and Turner, 2002d). Furthermore, in many developing countries, the private banking sector is not enthusiastic to introduce corporate governance principles. For example, in India, this problem can be summarised in the corporate sector as the privileging of the interests of one group over all other interests in a company.

Conclusion

Corporate governance in banking sector is being implemented under the guidance and regulations of SEBI and RBI. In India, Banking sector is facing some problems while implementing corporate governance. As most of the banks in India are protected by the government rules and regulations. The employees also somewhat negligent towards implementation of corporate governance. However, now all public sector banks are facing severe competition from private sector. In this context, the need for implementation of corporate governance in a systematic and strategic manner is becoming the need of the hour.

REFERENCES

1. Gilson, Stuart, Kose John and Larry Lang, 1990, "Troubled Debt Restructurings: An Empirical Study of Private Reorganization of Firms in Default", *Journal of Financial Economics*, Vol. 27, pp. 315-353.
2. *International Monetary Fund (IMF)*, 2001, "India: Recent Economic Developments and Selected Issues", IMF Country Report, No. 01/181.
3. Rajan, Raghuram G. and Luigi Zingales, 1998, "Financial Systems, Industrial Structure, and Growth", unpublished.
4. RBI and SEBI Guidelines.

10

Scams in Indian Capital Markets: Reflections on Corporate Governance

Prof. P. V. Sarma and T. V. V. Phani Kumar

Globalization helps in the integration of the world's financial markets across countries, which increases opportunity for the companies to raise funds globally. The capital markets facilitate the internationalisation of an economy by linking it with the rest of the world. This linkage assists through the inflow of capital. Moreover, a strong domestic stock market performance forms the basis for well performing domestic corporate to raise capital in the international market. It is also very likely that existence of a domestic securities market will discourage capital outflow by providing attractive investment opportunities within domestic economy. The scandals up to early 2000 in the capital market have underscored the role of corporate governance in protecting the interests of investors in India. However with the present vigilance system on Demat accounts, accumulation of stocks, check on number of transactions and code of governance is helping to detect the scams at the early stage (IPOs of Yes Bank, IDFC etc.) and reposing confidence in the investors and especially FIIs.

Capital Markets in India

Capital Markets are the means through which small and scattered savings of the investors are directed into productive activities of corporate entities. A well-organized and regulated capital market facilitates sustainable development of the economy by providing long-term funds in exchange of financial assets to investors. Indian capital market is one of the oldest and largest capital markets of the world. Its history can be traced back to the 19th century. The first instance of organized trading in corporate securities in India is related to the trading in securities of East India Company. In 1875, Dalal Street in Mumbai became prominent with the instigation of Bombay Stock Exchange (BSE), the first organized stock exchange in India. After Independence, the Indian Government gave priority to infrastructure development, considering the urgency of proceeding with large scale industrial development. In mid-eighties there was an impressive growth in the secondary markets as ten stock exchanges were established. In 1991, Government of India launched a policy of liberalization and globalization of Indian economy in general and of financial sector in particular. It covered measures like abolition of industrial licensing except for short list of industries, 51 per cent foreign ownership of equity, permission for Foreign Institutional Investors (FIIs) to invest in securities in primary and secondary market and permission for Indian companies to raise capital abroad through the issue of Global Depository Receipts (GDRs) or American Depository Receipts (ADRs). These reforms, particularly in financial sector, fuelled the growth of equity markets in India. A remarkable moment in the capital markets had taken place in the year 1992, with the incorporation of Securities and Exchange Board of India (SEBI) as a investor protection body by the virtue of a special enactment, namely the SEBI Act, 1992. The primary duty of the board is to protect the interest of investors in securities and to promote the development of and to regulate the capital market. In the past five years Indian capital market has begun to transform rapidly in order to provide world class services to the investors. A variety of developmental measures like deregulation and economic reforms, disintermediation and financial sector reforms, institutionalization of stock markets, investors preference for higher standards of disclosures and corporate governance in measures similar to those followed in developed markets, globalization and tax reforms etc., have all contributed to bring about the required changes in the capital market sense. These changes and reforms have been taken up in the best interest of all stakeholders of capital market.

Need for Corporate Governance

The financial capital flow across national borders creates necessity for the investors to ensure that the enterprises or the markets in which they are investing are not only managed competently that means they have good corporate management but also they are governed properly.

The collapse of the South East Asian tiger economies like Thailand, South Korea, Malaysia, Indonesia in 1998 brought home the fact that if there is no proper corporate governance in the financial sector, it leads to corruption. This, in turn, leads to unsound investments, which are speculative and finally the investors lose.

Corporate governance depends upon two factors. The first is the commitment of the management for the principle of integrity and transparency in business operations. The second is the legal and the administrative framework created by the government. If public governance is weak, we cannot have good corporate governance. The dramatic Enron case has highlighted how companies, which were the hot stocks of the stock market and held up as models for vigorous and innovative growth can ultimately collapse like a house of cards as they were based on fraud and dishonesty. In the Indian context, the need for corporate governance has been highlighted because of the scams we have been having almost as an annual feature ever since we had liberalization from 1991.

Corporate Governance Calls for Three Factors

(a) Transparency in decision-making,

(b) Accountability which follows from transparency because responsibilities could be fixed easily for actions taken or not taken, and

(c) The accountability is for the safeguarding the interests of the stakeholders and the investors in the organization.

Scams in Capital Markets

A simple record of the scams in the capital markets is presented below:

- *The securities scam of 1992:* This was the mother of all Indian financial scandals. It exposed the lawlessness and absence of supervision in the money markets; it allowed funds to be transferred with impunity from banks and corporate houses into the equity markets. A Special Court under a separate act of Parliament was set up and the CBI filed over 70 cases but not a single scamster has been finally convicted by the slow judicial system. Instead, their repeated attempts to re-enter the market with the same bag of tricks have caused further losses to investors.

- *The IPO bubble:* The entry of Foreign Institutional investors led to a massive bull run, which saw the secondary market recover from the scam even though *badla* was banned. Soon thereafter, the control over Capital Issues was abolished with a one-line order and it opened the floodgates for a massive scam in the primary market (or initial public offerings). This scam had two parts – the first was perpetrated by existing companies which ramped up their prices in order to raise money at hugely inflated premia to fund greenfield projects and mindless diversifications, most of which have either failed to take off or are languishing. The other half of the scam had a multitude of small traders, chartered accountants and businessmen, who teamed up with bankers and investment bankers to float new companies and raise public funds.The IPO bubble which lasted three years from 1993 to 1996 finally burst when prices of listed companies began to crash. So huge was investors' disappointment that the primary market remained dead for the next two years, almost until the beginning of 1999.
- *Preferential allotment rip-off:* This was an offshoot of the rampant price rigging on the secondary market. Apart from raising fresh funds, promoters of Indian companies who thought that prices would never come down, quickly orchestrated general body clearances to allot shares to themselves on a preferential basis and at a substantial discount to the market. Multinational companies such as Colgate and Castrol started the trend and it led to a benefit of nearly Rs. 5000 crores (in relation to market prices at that time) to retail investors before the Securities and Exchange Board of India (SEBI) put in place a set of rules to block the practice.
- *CRB's house of cards:* Chain Roop Bhansali's (CRB) cardboard empire is only the biggest and most audacious of many that were built and disappeared in the new 'liberalised' milieu of the mid-1990s. His Rs. 1000 crore financial conglomerate comprised of a mutual fund, fixed deposit collection, a merchant bank and a provisional banking license. Armed with these and favourable credit ratings and audit reports, CRB created a pyramid based on high cost financing which finally collapsed. The winner: C. R. Bhansali, who, after a

brief spot of trouble with the authorities moved on to the dot com business and the regulators who were never held accountable. The losers: millions of small investors who lost through fixed deposits or the mutual fund. The CRB collapse caused a run on other finance companies causing a huge systemic problem and further losses to investors.

- *Plantation companies' puffery:* These followed the same strategy as vanishing companies, and since they were subject to no regulation, could get away with wild profit projections. They positioned themselves as part mutual fund, part IPO and promised the most incredible returns – over 1000 per cent at least in seven years. High profile television campaigns, full-page advertisments and glossy brochures had the investors flocking for more. Almost all these projects, with barely any exception have vanished.
- *Mutual funds disaster:* Starting with the scam-hit Canstar scheme, most mutual funds had to be bailed out by their sponsor banks, or parent institutions. This came the big bail out of Unit Trust of India. Since UTI is set up under its own act, it was the tax-payers who paid for the Rs. 4800 crore bailout in 1999. Just three years later, it was back buying recklessly into the Ketan Parekh manipulated scrips and suffering big losses in the process. The record of the private mutual funds has also been inconsistent. It will be a long time indeed before small investors consider mutual funds a reasonably safe investment.
- *The 1998 collapse:* What could be a bigger indicator of the ineffectiveness of the regulatory system and the moral bankruptcy in the country than the return of Harshad Mehta? In 1998, he made a comeback by floating a website to hand out stock tips and writing columns in several newspapers who were told that his column would push up their circulation figures. His rigging of BPL, Videocon and Sterlite shares ended with the inevitable collapse and a cover up operation involving an illegal opening of the trading system in the middle of the night by the Bombay Stock Exchange officials. It cost the BSE President and Executive Director their jobs, but the broker and the companies have got away so far.

- *The K-10 gimmick:* This too is already on the way to be hushed up even before it is fully investigated. Though everybody knows this as a Ketan Parekh scandal, but if one examines the selective leak of the SEBI investigation report to the media, it would seem as though only three operators caused the problem by hammering down prices. The government promised stringent action not only against Ketan Parekh and the brokers who hammered down prices, but also the regulators who and companies/banks which planed with them to divert funds to the market.
- *The demat scam:* The Securities and Exchange Board of India (SEBI) has discovered yet another multiple demat account scam in 2005's IPO of Infrastructure Development Finance Company (IDFC), raising alarming questions about the oversight of demat accounts used by millions of investors. A SEBI probe, showed that about 8.29 per cent of the retail portion of the IDFC IPO amounting to Rs. 1.17 crore shares were received by fictitious applicants who operated multiple demat accounts. The players, who were also involved in the Yes Bank IPO demat scam, were found to have used the same modus operandi to corner large number of shares in highly successful IDFC issue. Roopalben Panchal, along with associates and other entities, cornered large chunks of IDFC shares by opening about 47,000 fictitious accounts. These accounts were opened with Karvy-DP, just like in the Yes Bank case.

Capital Market Regulatory System in India

SEBI, the Reserve Bank of India (RBI), and the Insurance Regulatory and Development Authority (IRDA) supervise India's equity markets. The Ministry of Company Affairs has the ultimate responsibility for ensuring compliance with the Companies Act of 1956. The capital market regulatory structure in India is illustrated as shown p. 86.

As Data clearly shows that the Coefficient of variation increases from A to B1 and from B1 to B2. Further, it is highest in Z . This clearly indicates that the investment in Z-category of companies is riskier when compared to other groups and investment in B2 securities is also risk prone.

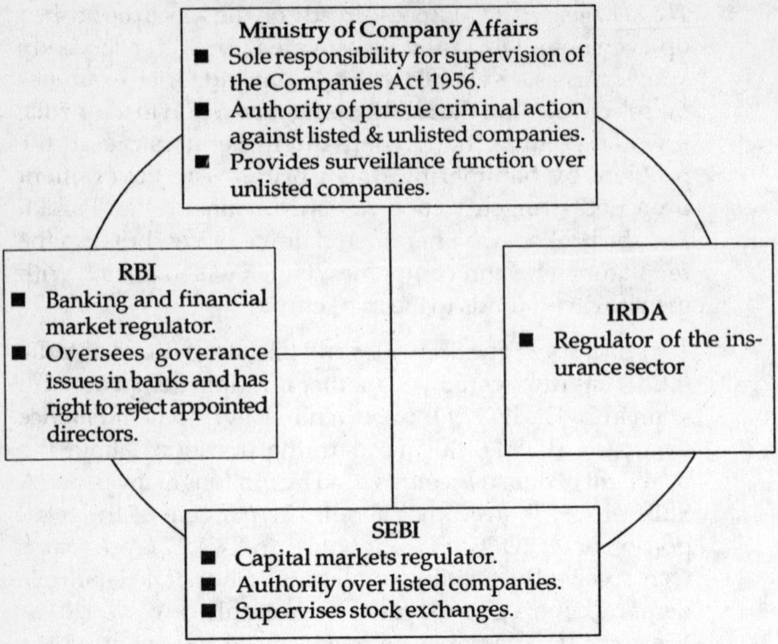

Analysis of Turnover of Different Category of Scrips at Bombay Stock Exchange

(Rs. in Crores)

Year	*A Group*	*B1 Group*	*B2 Group*	*S Group*	*T Group*	*Z- Group*
Jan-05	30423.61	10517.63	952.27	918.45	931.56	132.61
Feb-05	30819.34	13871.33	1328.68	2157.73	1331.04	162.08
Mar-05	39168.75	14556.41	1331.02	2521.69	1575.29	358.99
Apr-05	23352.51	11270.61	1148.04	1540.81	413.35	72.46
May-05	23851.18	13747.38	2381.13	2672.87	544.33	146.69
Jun-05	35140.29	15230.01	3060.79	3767.79	1061.34	199.28
Jul-05	32892.14	20080.71	3472.04	4037.08	1180.71	210.37
Aug-05	39724.42	22122.01	5648.11	5770.46	2228.57	411.47
Sep-05	39241.98	27195.13	5822.03	6380.59	2276.16	351.04
Oct-05	43044.23	11430.01	1515.48	2438.09	590.94	60.57
Nov-05	36772.54	11729.19	1230.89	2386.45	505.46	49.49
Dec-05	48540.46	21176.06	2783.31	4164.75	597.45	67.47

(Contd.)

Year	*A Group*	*B1 Group*	*B2 Group*	*S Group*	*T Group*	*Z- Group*
Mean	35247.62	16077.21	2556.217	3229.858	1103.047	185.03
SD	7452.864	5308.763	1700.429	1642.935	647.9459	126.1767
Coefficient of Variation	0.211443	0.330204	0.665213	0.508671	0.587415	0.680932

Analysis of Dividend Payout of Different Category of Scrips at Bombay Stock Exchange

Out of 9644 listed companies, as per SEBI's count, the BSE has provided a break-up of 6330 of its own listed companies as follows: A-Group = 200; B-1 Group = 800; B-2 Group = 1830 and Z Group = 3500. The Z group comprises companies which are not complying with listing rules. A new group called "T" (companies under surveillance) was carved out a few months ago. The boundary lines among these groups go on changing as companies are transferred by the BSE from one group to another.

It is interesting to note that the percentage of dividend-paying companies systematically falls as we proceed from A to Z group: A-Group = 91.2 per cent; B-1 Group = 62.8 per cent; B-2 Group = 24.3 per cent; T-Group = 16.5 per cent; and Z-Group = 5.9 per cent. Our analysis bestows a special significance to the classification of companies into the various listed groups. Hitherto, this classification was regarded only as reflecting the difference in market liquidity among the groups.

Measures to Protect Investors of Capital Markets

The following measures are suggestible for protecting the investors in the capital market:

- Strengthen Clause 49 by giving SEBI and stock exchanges the authority to take action against errant companies (besides de-listing) by substantially increasing the cost of non-compliance.
- A mechanism should be developed to control the price fluctuations of the stocks at the time of listing. No investor should be allowed to sell more than 20 per cent of the total allotted shares for one year from the date of listing.
- A unique social security number should be allocated to all

the citizens of the country, wherein any financial transactions should be allowed after providing the security code only.

- Improve surveillance mechanisms by adding manpower and training existing staff in the surveillance function at the stock exchange and regulatory authority level to carry out more compliance audits.
- Improve corporate governance-related reporting by companies to include back-up information to explain compliance with key requirements of Clause 49.
- A system should be developed to charge short-term capital gains at the time of transfer of shares.

Conclusion

Corporate governance has become a highly significant and relevant concept in the context of globalisation. Turning the rhetoric of corporate governance into reality depends on two players, the leaders of business units and the government. Significant government action is needed to improve the enforcement and surveillance functions of regulators in India. All these will ensure proper corporate governance and protect the Indian capital market investors.

REFERENCES

Sucheta Dalal, *"10 years of financial scams", an article at* www.suchetadalal.com.

Task Force Report on *" Corporate Governance in India – An Investors' Perspective"*, submitted by Institute of International Finance, February 2005.

N. Vittal, *"Issues in corporate governance in India"*, paper presented in 5th JRD Tata Memorial Lecture Series.

A Research Report on *"Corporate Governance and Market Reactions"*, by Vijaya B Marisetty and A.V. Vedpuriswar.

Jayanth Rama Varma, *"Corporate Governance in India : Disciplining Dominant Shareholder"*, IIMB Management Review, October-December 1997, pp 5-18.

Gupta, L.C. *"Stock Exchange Trading in India : Agenda for Reform"*, Society for Capital Market Research and Development, Delhi,1992, p. 123s.

11

Values and Ethics in Business Basis for Corporate Governance

S. Rajani and Mrs. D. Jyotsna Rani

Cadbury is no longer sweeter to many Corporates since December 1992, when a Committee led by Sir Adrian Cadbury submitted its report on Corporate Governance in the US. The report of this committee has activated the Corporate Governance movement in India as well. Corporate Governance is on the cards due to the following reasons:

- Significant increase in the number of shareholders who expect international standards in the governance of enterprises.
- Banks and financial institutions, which are now being subjected to strict accounting norms, have started focusing on enhanced corporate performance.

Corporate Governance is no longer just corporate management. It is something much broader and includes major parameters of accountability, control, transparency and reporting system in the governance of corporations. It is therefore said that Corporate Governance is a process or system to ensure that the company is managed in the best interest of all the stakeholders. Some of the underlying *principles of Corporate Governance* are as follows:

- It must allow shareholders to buy and sell shares freely.
- It must maintain balanced accountability to all the stakeholders i.e., not preferential accountability to a particular stakeholder group.
- It should reflect the economic and social culture of the country concerned.

- It must essentially establish a network of accountability relationship between Board of Directors, Shareholders and Auditors.
- It should strive to achieve the right balance between shareholders and management.

The Companies Act, 1956 provides a formal structure of Corporate Governance, which assures the accountability relation between Board of Directors, Shareholders and Auditors. The composition and structural balance of Board of Directors is the most important element of Corporate Governance. The Kumara Mangalam Birla Committee recommends that the Board of a company have an optimum combination of executive and non-executive directors with not less than 50 per cent of Board comprising non-executive Directors. In case a company has non-executive Chairman, at least 1/3rd should comprise independent Directors and if it has an executive Chairman, half of the Board should be independent. These are mandatory recommendations of the committee. Besides there should also be nominees from financial or investment institutions to safeguard the interests of the shareholders.

Corporate Governance and Ethics

The concept of Corporate Governance is not new to Indian business. In Arthasastra some concepts mentioned by Kautilya tally with current global consensus of good Corporate Governance. "Sukhasya moolam dharma" means root of all happiness is doing right; "dharmasya moolam artha" means root of doing right is the root of wealth;"arthasya moolam rajyam" means root of wealth is Enterprise. In Gandhian philosophy, the principle of "trusteeship" also tells us that the corporates should not maximize profits at the cost of society, the social motive should be given over-riding priority. The core theme of late Pt. Jawaharlal Nehru on public enterprises was centralized basically that these enterprises should be established to achieve the goal of serving the masses living in our society—the economic priorities should be designed in such a way that they can help achieve the goal of self-reliance. The president of BSE Mr. Anand Rathi has said that the time has come now to take action against non-performing or errant companies. He believes that the investors have the right to know about the quality of the listed companies. The Industrial Policy 1991 paved the way and made the Corporate Governance entry easy globally.

Business Enterprise is a social institution created by men. It can't keep itself aloof from this syndrome. In spite of all the codes, laws, rules etc., business has been milking the mother earth ruthlessly. Optimum utilization of resources is one of the main objectives of any firm. Corporate Governance is commonly perceived as not simply a matter of creating an outer performing organization, which strives towards maximizing customer satisfaction and shareholder value. For this a corporate culture has to be created; the responsibility of creating such culture lies on the Board of Directors who should become effective pilots of management rather that confining themselves to statutory functions alone. The employees must not only speak of empowerment but must also accept the accompanying responsibility. There is nothing radical about the concept of Corporate Governance—it has been developed and practiced by corporations both here at home and abroad with sustained success.

Though the codes for Corporate Governance were formulated by and large by the developed countries, these are not new to India. About 5000 yrs back, "Manusmrithi" prescribed a detail code of conduct for society. However as years passed, we find a gradual shift away from prescriptions, thus increasing the gap between what is desirable and what is actually practiced.

Sudden Heightened Interest in Corporate Governance

- Assertion of rights by shareholders.
- Significant presence of foreign institutions. Investors who are demanding greater professionalism in management of Indian corporations.
- Concern on the part of lending institutions about the performance of the companies financed by them.
- Integration of India with the world economy, which demands that Indian industry, conforms to the standard set of international rules and norms.

According to a recent report, financial fraud is the most rapidly growing problem that is being faced by the Indian business community today. The report states that around 14,000 cases of financial fraud involving more than Rs. 2000 crores worth of assets had occurred in Public Sector banks during the period 1998-2005.

The RBI also reported 592 cases of fraud in foreign banks involving funds worth Rs. 14.66 crores.

However, the Indian Banks' case, reporting a mammoth loss of Rs. 1336 crores figured as a major scandal. The loss is the highest ever recorded by an Indian banks till date. This apart, the banks had around Rs. 2000 crores in the form of non-performing assets. In 1994-95, the Banks had reported a capital adequacy of 8.5 per cent. It now has its entire net worth wiped out. The Supreme Court declared that CBI and other government agencies had failed to perform their statutory functions by not fully investigating the Indian Bank loan fraud. Recently a number of cases were lodged in the court of law relating to financial fraud by some Non-Banking Financial Companies.

As many as 2500 out of 3900 companies listed between 1991-96 have completely disappeared. More than 100 dot com companies flatted in India have vanished from the scene. A number of NBFCs have run away with hard earned money of investors.

However, Corporate Governance is not a tailor–made programme, which has universal applicability to all at all times. Each company can select and adopt its own mode of Corporate Governance keeping in view the relationship among Board of Directors– Shareholders–Auditors.

Therefore, the Theory of Corporate Governance rests on four major principles:

- Sound management practices leading to increased Return On Investment.
- Fiduciary relationship between Board of Directors–Shareholders–Auditors.
- The companies must refrain from unethical practices and think in terms of protecting natural resources and societal wealth as a whole.
- Fulfilling the role that Gandhiji termed as "Trusteeship". Transparency in the overall working of organisation.

Examples of Corporate Governance Failures

The cases of Enron and World com debacles have drawn consideration to the argument favouring strengthening of corporate governance framework worldwide. The recent examples of Parmalat in Italy.

Enron Case

Scandal, secrecy, misleading information, inaccurate financial reporting – all in a day's work for WorldCom and Enron, two of the world's most corrupt and bankrupt companies. That employees and investors alike have suffered extraordinary economic losses at the hands of company executives whose own coat pockets were lined quite nicely prior to the breach of wrong-doing speaks to a sector of society that has placed the bottom line far, far before any ethical or social consideration.

What happened at Enron and the role that it appears that auditing firm Arthur Andersen played? The Enron story is still unfolding and we do not yet know the extent of the damage of the company's collapse, but former investors already are suing for a litany of reasons using a variety of synonyms for the dreaded "f" word, meaning fraud. It appears that we will be hearing a lot of that word in coming months as the story continues to unfold.

Enron was named as the most innovative corporation in America for six straight years by Fortune Magazine. In late 2001, however, the S&P had downgraded Enron stock to junk status. What happened? This is the topic of this paper. Diversification, conflicts of interest, unethical operations, and misrepresentations – these all played a part in the devastation of Enron Corporation.

The Enron debacle clearly illustrates how establishing and maintaining corporate ethics is the cornerstone to continued success, both on a personal and professional level. Constant nurturing of moral judgment and a specific code of ethics are necessary in order to perpetuate the positive image required to uphold such policy. The five primary elements of such nurturing include having a clear and concise forthrightness, which is substantiated by culture; appropriate and applicable conformity with regard to difficult situations; managerial involvement and awareness on ethics issues; a nurturing programme that is wholeheartedly supported by top management; and staff involvement. These concepts, which are both interrelated and individual at the same time, represent a complete quest toward ethical decision-making.

The Enron collapse is an example of misleading financial reporting. Enron concealed huge losses by creating illusions that a third party was contractually obliged to pay the amount of any losses. However, the third party was an entity in which Enron had a substantial economic stake. In discussions of accounting practices with the partner Anderson in-charge of auditing, views inevitably led to the client prevailing.

Enron executives clearly harbored their own personal agendas when it was finally discovered how their unethical behaviour was responsible for the company's downfall, which only served to ultimately and completely compromise whatever integrity it may have established over the years.

The developments within Enron in terms of the ethical and moral justification in the choices corporate executives make in life when they have different agendas from that of their companies. John Stewart Mill's theory of utilitarianism and Immanuel Kant's categorical imperative of reason are of particular benefit in this ethical examination.

Discussing the ethical failures associated with Enron's collapse. There were many problems at Enron, but the largest and most devastating lay with its use of Special Purpose Entities (SPEs). Enron and its auditor, Arthur Andersen, abandoned ethical behaviour with equal enthusiasm.

Enron's approach to conflict management during its collapse fiasco. Regardless of what is found later to be at the root of all the problems that the company faces now, even the most superficial glance at the company illustrates that it does not operate under effective principles of conflict management. At the very time that the company most needs to operate as a cohesive unit, individuals at all levels are pointing fingers in all sorts of directions.

The failure of Enron from an accounting perceptive. The causes of the collapse are identified as ranging between auditing issues, such as independence, accounting issues including the way that special purpose entities (SPEs) were used to conceal losses, corporate governance attitudes and structures, pensions, banking issues, and derivative issues. However, good financial reporting is not a sufficient condition for the effectiveness of corporate governance if users don't process it, or if the informed user is unable to exercise a monitoring role due to high costs.

Worldcom

Worldcom was a leading telecommunications industry which was doing extremely well in the 1990s. However, shortly after the MCI acquisition in 1998, the telecommunications industry entered a downturn and Worldcom's growth strategy suffered a serious blow when it was forced to abandon its proposed merger with Sprint in late 2000. By that time, Worldcom's stock was declining and its CEO Bernard Ebbers came under increasing pressure from banks to cover margin calls on his Worldcom stock that was used to finance his other businesses (timber and yachting, among others). During 2001, Ebbers persuaded Worldcom's board of directors to provide him corporate loans and guarantees in excess of $ 400 million to cover his margin calls, but this strategy ultimately failed and Ebbers was ousted as CEO in April 2002 and replaced by John Sigmore.

Beginning in 1999 and continuing through May 2002, the company used fraudulent accounting methods to mask its declining financial condition by painting a false picture of financial growth and profitability to prop up the price of Worldcom's stock. The fraud was accomplished primarily in two ways: (1) underreporting 'line costs' (interconnection expenses with other telecommunication companies) by capitalizing these costs on the balance sheet rather than properly expensing them and (2) inflating revenues with bogus accounting entries from 'corporate unallocated revenue accounts.' Worldcom's internal audit department uncovered approximately $ 3.8 billion of the fraud in June 2002 during a routine examination of capital expenditures and alerted the company's new auditors, KPMG.

Parmalat

Parmalat SpA an Italian dairy and food corporation and Europe's biggest dairy company was declared bankrupt in 2003. One of the biggest scandals in Italian history came to light as a 8 billion hole was discovered in Parmalat's accounting records.The company was charged with financial fraud and money laundering. Among the questionable accounting practices used by Parmalat, it sold itself credit-linked notes, in effect placing a bet on its own credit worthiness in order to conjure up an asset out of thin air. The CEO reported having diverted funds from Parmalat into Parmatour (sports and tourism venture) and elsewhere.

Values and Ethics in Business

In all the above cases two things appear to be on the forefront—Business ethics and individual values of people in power in the various institutions. Hence, the fundamental cause for lapses in corporate governance in spite of the systems, rules and norms is the failure on part of the human behaviour in terms of values and ethics. This may be one of the reasons for the relatively less number of lapses on corporate governance in the Asian countries where traditionally the principles of ethics and values are strongly engraved in the society. Therefore, there is a need to establish a link between ethics and corporate governance.

"What you are is God's gift to you while what you become is your (return) gift to God."

Interest in the above saying is the question of values and ethics in all walks of life. These words in the recent times have become ubiquitous and hence ambiguous. The word "Value" is derived from French "VALOIR" which means worth, merit, usefulness or importance of a thing. Value is not something absolute but is considered in comparison to something else. It is a behavioural concept related to an individual or a group. A value is a concept of desirable worth which influences the choices of available means and ends. One's choice of a course of action is dependent on value alternatives. We could define Value as "an enduring belief that a specific mode of conduct or end state of existence is personally or socially preferable to an opposite or converse mode of conduct or end state of existence."

Values and Organization

Values are relevant to an individual because all his/her actions, choices, options are dependent on his/her set of values. An individual perception, attitude, behaviour and judgments are all influenced by his/her set of values.

Therefore to an Organization, values are:

- A major determinant of managerial and organizational effectiveness.

- Key to ensure optimum results.
- Help in fostering spirit of mutual trust, confidence and higher commitment.
- Assist in building resilience against failures and adapting to environmental changes.
- Help in achieving greater cohesion and loyalty.

Ethics—A View Point

The word *Ethics* is derived from Greek term *ethos* meaning a system of moral principles, the basis to decide "right and wrong" actions mainly emphasizing on the spirit of culture or the disposition *vasanas.* On the other hand, Ethics denotes a set of codes of behaviour, which sustain mutual confidence. Ethics represents moral principles, judgements/actions.

Termed as ethical or unethical depending upon their value content. Interest in the subject of Business Ethics has grown dramatically during second half of 20th century. Business executives, academicians and general public have come to appreciate economic reasoning and ethical judgement.

The Ethics of Corporate Governance is therefore determination of what is "right, fair, proper and just" in decisions and actions that affect other people. It focuses on what our relationships are and ought to be—with our employees, customers, stockholders, creditors, suppliers, distributors, neighbours and other members of community/society in which we operate.

Conclusion

The emergence of new corporate governance norms will decide the direction of Indian market and the motivational level of new and existing entrepreneurs will be a force to be reckoned with. Undoubtedly the market is becoming globally competitive information technology is becoming a reckoning force, the government has to provide a conducive environment both for private as well as public sector undertakings. Corporate governance in India has to decide the level of private sector participation in industries. It has to formulate modus operandi for disinvestments of loss making PSEs. It has to further ensure a proper and judicious use of sources coming out of the disinvestments process. The new CG has to provide a fresh look to all important industrial laws in India such as the

MRTP, FEMA, Company's Act etc. The most significant aspect of a new and desirable CG is to boost the inflow of foreign capital to India. To streamline the inflow, corporate governance has to ensure all sorts of facilities to foreigner investors. A strong institutional set-up with minimum bureaucratic bottlenecks, infrastructure development and political support are crucial factors along with other things.

12

Corporate Governance—Implications to Indian Business

Prof. J. V. Prabhakara Rao and Dr. S. Rajani

Corporate Governance, a phase that not long ago meant little to all, but a handful of scholars and shareholders, has now become a mainstream concern—a staple of discussion in Boardrooms, academic fora and policy circles worldwide. Two events may be considered to be responsible for the heightened interest in Corporate Governance.

- Financial Crisis of 1998 in Russia, Asia and Brazil.
- Corporate Governance scandles in 2001-03 in United States Europe which triggered off some of the largest insolvencies in the Global History.

Both these incidents brought to focus how the behaviour of corporate sectors could effect entire economies and endanger the stability of global financial systems.

In the aftermath, not only has the phrase Corporate Governance become almost a household term, but economists, policy makers and corporate world everywhere began to recognise the lurking macro-economic consequences of weak corporate Governance systems.

Underlying Reasons for Increased Attention to Corporate Governance

- Increasing size of the firms and the role of financial intermediaries and institutional investors in fund raising. The process of capital mobilisation has increasingly become one step removed from the principal owner.

- Allocation of capital has become more complex since investment choices have increased with liberalization of financial and real markets.
- Structural reforms like price de-regulation and intensified competition increased Companies' vulnerability to market forces.
- Increased levels of awareness among the stakeholders viz. employees, shareholders, creditors, suppliers, customers etc. which has to lead to greater levels of accountability and responsibility.

Corporations generally work within a framework of Governance which is set by law by regulation by corporations' own constitution, by those who own and fund them and by the expectations of those they serve. This framework differs from country to country since it depends to a large extent on the history and culture of the particular country. Corporate Governance therefore represents the value framework, ethical and moral framework under which business decisions are taken. Countries and corporations are advised to start from where they are and to build on their existing structures or systems instead of borrowing these from foreign countries.

Corporate Governance therefore calls for four basic principles to be adhered to—fairness, transparency, accountability and responsibility. These principles are equally relevant to privately run, public sector, state owned or widely held businesses. Private capital, in the recent times has become a prime source of funds for investment, which is usually handled by intermediaries who look for equal spread of risk and return. This once again reiterates the significance of corporate governance. The more widely these principles are applied, the better are the chances for equitable and effective allocation of resources. When companies are open and transparent about their plans and purposes, they stand better chances of winning the trust of the investors. Resources flow faster into companies, which inspire trust, through their approach to Corporate Governance. Example HDFC is one of the highly rated companies on Corporate Governance in India and this has helped to attract tremendous response to its public issue.

Similarly, best employee practices in terms of transparency in recruitment, promotions and adequate focus on career planning has put companies like Infosys and Wipro on the top of ratings related to employee management.

In other words, Corporate Governance is a continuous process. In its broadest sense it is concerned with striking balance between economic and social goals and also between individual and communal aspirations. The basic objective of the Corporate Governance, according to Adrian Cadbury is to align as nearly as possible the interests of individuals of Corporations and of society. What does each of the above get in return?

- Corporations which adopt internationally accepted governance standards are able to attract better investment and achieve their aims faster.
- The nation tends to benefit because these standards help to strengthen their economies and encourage business probability.
- Individuals benefit by a better standard of life and qualitative living through increased access to information at all levels.

Direct Implications of Corporate Governance on the Company

Increased access to external financing at lower cost. This leads to larger investment, higher growth, greater employment creation.

- The lower cost of capital results in the long-run, in higher firm valuation. This makes investment more attractive to investors leading to higher growth and more employment.
- Good Corporate Governance is associated with a reduced risk of financial lapses which can have large economic and social costs.
- Ensuring better operational performance through better allocation of resources and prudent management helps create more wealth for the company.
- It also helps in forging better relationships with all stakeholders like employees, general public and shareholders.

Governance Catalysts within Companies

A firm's response to Corporate Governance is likely to be determined by a combination of factors like:

- Ownership and management structure (example family controlled and managed versus family controlled and professionally managed).
- Degree of exposure to international competition for capital, customers and talent.
- Status as an independent company or part of a group.
- Nature of the Sector (Ex. high risk and new versus low risk and well established).
- Managerial Culture (orientation of senior managers towards Corporate Governance).

Corporate Governance in Developing Economies

Though issues relating to Corporate Governance are being hotly debated in the US and Europe over the last two decades, in the developing countries these have not been taken too seriously. In fact there is also a debate going on whether Corporate Governance is as important for developing countries where the national economies are dominated largely by family-owned, state owned or foreign investor owned companies that do not have shares widely traded on local stock markets; and where a number of small non- corporate firms often account for a significant proportion of local employment and output. Though the incidence of scattered financial scams has increased cautiousness among corporates, it has not acquired the seriousness that it ought to. Corporate Governance continues to be seen by many as relatively unimportant in developing countries largely because of paucity of firms with widely traded shares and employment of local people. The poor quality of local systems of Corporate Governance lies at the heart of one of the greatest challenges that most of the developing countries face today and how to transform the local systems of economic and political governance including corporate governance from systems that tend to be highly personalized and thus strongly relationship based, into systems that are more effectively rules based.

Indian Scenario

India is no exception; Corporate Governance did not receive much attention in the initial phase of the post-1991 reform period. Since India had inherited a rules-based system from Britain, there had been only steady improvement in laws relating to rules-based governance. The quality of financial and non- financial disclosures, mandated by law, are stronger in India when compared to a number of developing and developed countries (World Bank, 2000). However, the recent development in the financial sector has led to increased competitiveness and greater focus on Corporate Governance.Public financial institutions are now going to the capital market to meet their capital needs, foreign institutional investors have acquired a significant stake in the Indian financial system. All this has made it necessary for the Indian Corporates to focus on greater transparency and accountability.

In India implementation of Corporate Governance has largely been based on the Kumara Mangalam Birla code, and the CII code for Corporate Governance. However, codes can only provide guidelines. Ultimately effective Corporate Governance depends on the commitment of the people in the organization. The quantity, quality and frequency of financial and managerial responsibilities toward shareholders, the quality of information that management shares with their Boards, and the commitment to run transparent companies maximizes long-term shareholder value. In Asia, India ranks third after Singapore and Hong Kong in terms of effectiveness of Corporate Governance.

Good Corporate Governance offers the promise of several benefits to Indian corporate, sector:

- A large number of foreign portfolio investors would come to India if satisfied with the transparency and disclosure standards adopted here. This is what happened in US in early 1980's and in UK in early 1990's.
- In the near future foreign pension funds will enter India in a big way. Since these firms hold onto to their stocks for longer time, their fund mangers look for better Corporate Governance.
- Indian financial institutions will not continue to support the management irrespective of performance. Instead they will convert their outstanding debt into equity, set up merger and acquisition subsidiaries and sell their shares to more dynamic entrepreneurs.
- Improve chances of Indian Financial Institutions to go for GDRs, External Commercial Borrowings and Private placements.

- Financial press will become stronger with greater access to information.
- Will pave the path for introducing full capital account convertibility for the Indian rupee.

Conclusion

Therefore, it may be said that Corporate Governance means relatively more to India than many other countries since it is on the steep path of economic progress and Corporate Governance can be an important vehicle to traverse this journey. In fact good governance, not specific to any special sector is the need of the hour. Some of the issues that need to be emphasized on for Indian companies to achieve competence at global levels are:

Priorities for Regulators

- Increased concentration on enforcement rather than mere focus on models.
- Greater levels of convergence of local and international standards.
- Facilitating both financial and marketing discipline.
- Managing cross–border issues.

Priorities for Investors

- Strengthening and implementation of shareholder rights.
- Pre- emption rights, Meetings' attendance.
- Proxy voting.

Priorities for Companies

- Getting the basics right—accountability structures must receive more attention.
- Focus must be on fundamental best practices (rather than whistles and bells).

REFERENCE

N. Vittal, "Issues in Corporate Governance in India", paper presented in 5th JRD Tata Memorial Lecture Series.

13

Corporate Governance—Impact on Asset Allocation Practices of Household Investors

P.V. Rao and T. V. V. Phani Kumar

Investors are the backbone of capital market. A developing economy, like India, needs a growing amount of investor savings to flow to corporate enterprises. The investors' asset allocation practices depend on their risk bearing capacity .The average returns from the bank deposits are five per cent p.a. and returns from the assured post office schemes like PPF, NSC, Post Office deposits are slightly higher over this. The other options available for the household investors are company deposits that offer 4-6 per cent interest depending on their safety ratings. On the other hand, most of the companies listed on stock exchanges offered returns more than 100 per cent in the previous. In the light of the above observations, it is evident that the equity investments are expected to play a major role in the process of asset allocation. At this juncture, it is the role of the regulatory authorities to protect the interests of the small investors in the capital market. The Securities and Exchange Board of India (SEBI), the independent capital markets regulator, has made significant efforts in this regard to keep up with changing corporate governance practices. In this paper, the changing asset allocation practices of the household investors in the era of corporate governance were discussed.

Need for Asset Allocation

Asset allocation is an investment portfolio technique that aims to balance risk and create diversification by dividing assets among major categories such as bonds, stocks, real estate, and cash. Each asset class has different levels of return and risk, so each will behave differently over time. At the same time that one asset is increasing in value, another may be decreasing or not increasing as much. The underlying principle of asset allocation is that the older a person gets, the lesser the risk he or she should face. The age of the investor has a positive impact on the asset allocation process. The investor of a lesser age allocates his savings in a risky investments whereas an investor of higher age allocates his savings in less risky investments. Therefore one must change asset allocation over time to move more towards safer asset classes (bonds, treasuries) as one gets older.

Risk Return Tradeoff

The return offered by different assets depends on their risk class. Low risks are generally associated with low potential returns. High risks are generally associated with high potential returns. The risk/return tradeoff is an effort to achieve a balance between the desire for the lowest possible risk and the highest possible return. This is demonstrated graphically in the chart below:

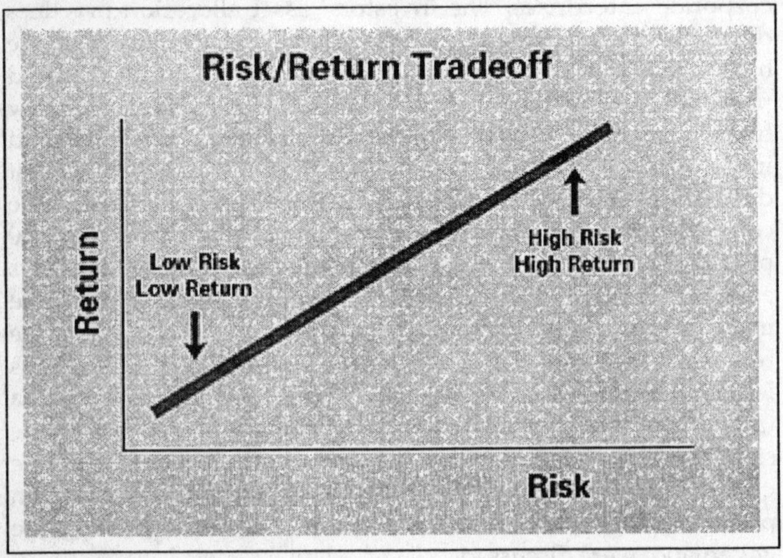

In the process of asset allocation, the investor selects the assets in the portfolio in such a manner so as to minimize the risk and to achieve maximum return.

Asset Allocation of Household Investors

The allocation of financial savings in financial and physical assets from 1991-2004 is illustrated in the following table:

Year	*Financial Assets*	*Physical Assets*	*Total*
1991-92	62101 (56%)	48635 (44%)	110736
1992-93	65367 (50%)	65706 (50%)	131073
1993-94	94738 (60%)	63572 (40%)	158310
1994-95	120733 (61%)	78625 (39%)	199358
1995-96	105719 (49%)	110421 (51%)	216140
1996-97	141661 (61%)	91591 (39%)	233252
1997-98	146777 (55%)	121660 (45%)	268437
1998-99	180346 (55%)	146456 (45%)	326802
1999-2000	205743 (51%)	198658 (49%)	404401
2000-01	216774 (48%)	235494 (52%)	452268
2001-02	253964 (49%)	259146 (51%)	513110
2002-03	254439 (44%)	320242 (56%)	574681
2003-04	314261 (47%)	357431 (53%)	671692

The percentage of savings in the financial assets has been fluctuating during the study period. The burst of the IPO bubble in the year 1996 badly effected the percentage of savings in financial assets i.e., the savings has decreased from 61 per cent in 1996-97 to 51 per cent in 1999-2000. Again with a new scam of Ketan Parekh bailed out in the year 2000 significantly effected the asset allocation process. With the SEBI taking stringent measures against the persons involved in the frauds in the capital market is able to retain the faith of the small investors towards financial assets in general and towards equity instruments in specific.

Role of Corporate Governance

India's equity markets are well developed compared to other emerging market countries. The Securities and Exchange Board of India (SEBI), an independent judicial body, regulates the exchanges. Corporate governance-related listing requirements in India are largely based on recommendations of the Cadbury and Higgs Reports and the Sarbanes-Oxley Act. SEBI has been proactive in keeping India's corporate governance rules and regulations in line with best practices around the world. In 1999, SEBI appointed the Kumara Mangalam Birla Committee to recommend improvements to the corporate governance framework. In 2002, SEBI updated its listing requirements with Clause 49, which has mandatory and non-mandatory corporate governance provisions. These listing requirements were again changed in 2004 to incorporate some best practices laid out in the Sarbanes-Oxley Act.

Measures to be Taken to Strengthen the Faith of Household Investors on Capital Markets

The following measures were suggested for the improvement of the faith of the investors in the capital market:

- Strengthen Surveillance system.
- Impose heavy fines on the companies which fail to meet the corporate governance code.
- Increase Investors awareness towards their rights in the capital markets.
- Ensure compliance of exciting standards with the listing standards on corporate governance of leading stock exchanges.
- Introduce sector specific corporate listing practices.

Conclusion

The state of corporate governance in India has improved over the last four years, particularly among large cap Indian companies. Improvements in corporate governance include increased transparency with regard to accounting and financial information and, to a lesser extent, more independent directors on boards. The Securities and Exchange Board of India (SEBI), is also making significant efforts to protect the small investors in the capital market and thereby encouraging them to invest their savings in equity.

REFERENCES

Task Force Report on *Corporate Governance in India—An Investors' Perspective*, submitted by Institute of International Finance, February 2005.

N. Vittal, *Issues in Corporate Governance in India*, paper presented in 5th JRD Tata Memorial Lecture Series.

A Research Report on *Corporate Governance and Market Reactions*, by Vijaya B. Marisetty and A.V. Vedpuriswar.

N. Gopalaswamy, *Corporate Governance—The New Paradigm*, Wheeler Publishing, A Division of A.H. Wheeler and Co. Ltd., New Delhi, 1998.

Barua, S. K. and Srinivasan G (1991), *Experiment on Individual Investment Decision Making Process, Sankhya*, Vol. 53, Series B, pp. 74-88.

Madhusudhan K. (2001), *Investment Behaviour of Household Sector—A Study of a Rural Block in West Bengal, The Indian Journal of Commerce*, Vol. 54, No.1 and 2, pp. 58-65.

14

Corporate Governance and Information Technology

P. Pinakapani and Dr. K. S. Bose

Introduction

In the post liberalization era, the economy is showing positive growth indicators and at the same time a word is often in the news—"Corporate Governance" mean the beliefs, values, culture and ethics, an interplay between individual aspirations and corporate goals in every functional aspects of an organization are binded or controlled together resulting in transparency and accountability of decisions and operations undertaken by the organization.

Introduction of a culture of Corporate Governance is the need of the hour for the comfort of all the stakeholders. The Ministry of Company Affairs (MCA), after consultations with Industry Associations and Professional Institutes, has set up Nation Foundation for Corporate Governance (NFCG) as a not-for-profit trust to provide a platform for deliberations on issues relating to good corporate governance and to sensitize corporate leaders on the importance of good corporate governance practices, self-regulation and directorial responsibilities. The Ministry has constituted the Governing Council under the Chairmanship of Minister for Company Affairs and has also launched a web site of the Foundation, which is expected to serve as a medium for policies for better corporate governance.

More specifically, corporate governance covers issues like:

- *(a)* The legal rights of financiers, the role of large investors,
- *(b)* The method of electing boards of directors,
- *(c)* The composition of the board, the ability of the board to maintain surveillance,

(*d*) The system of checks and balances instituted over managerial behaviour,

(*e*) The incentives offered to managers to protect financiers from dissipation of capital,

(*f*) The standards of financial reporting and corporate disclosure, and so on.

Information Technology and Corporate Governance

Security-related incidents have been on the front-burner of organizations for several years. Security breaches may occur due to the negligence of staffers, third-party access to key applications, or lack of appropriate security of information systems. It is essential that all organizations have information security policies and procedures in place as well as a formal incident response management team that can detect and escalate security breaches. Key risk areas that need to be focused in logical access management include lack of procedures on user access rights and inadequate review of access rights on a periodic basis. Segregation of duties amongst users should be addressed to promote tighter control. Physical access risks exist on account of poor awareness levels and training. Investments made by organizations are for physical goods and not on IT assets, especially data. Physical security functions are typically not integrated with information systems security.

Data integrity risk encompasses all of the risks associated with the authorization, completeness and accuracy of transactions as they are entered into, processed by, summarized and reported on by various application systems deployed by an organization. These risks pervasively apply to each and every aspect of an application system used in supporting a business process. Integrity can be lost due to programming and processing errors, and poor management. Adequate preventive controls and detection need to be put in place to ensure that only valid and complete data are entered into all systems and applications.

With IT there's a choice: you can drive it or be driven. In a business context, risk is not just about disasters and security attacks, but also about the business risks of costly project failures. Given the significant costs and strategic value of IT, measuring its performance is as important as any other key business function. Yet many organizations find IT performance measurement challenging, so they settle for measuring what they can rather than what they want or need to. Most organizations run several IT projects rather than an IT programme. Several of them are in fact 'Project Failures,' and this happens due to a number of reasons from poor planning to a weak business case, a lack of involvement from the top management, poor budgeting and inadequate quality control. With a significant amount of investment going into IT projects, failures can have adverse effects which can take months and years to recover from.

IT Strategy and Spends

Sub-optimal spending on IT can worsen the overall risk posture of an organization. Good IT governance includes the understanding of cost drivers and issues in IT, the nature of budgets and spending, and how spending is monitored. With IT costs increasing as a proportion of corporate expenditure, shareholders and other stakeholders expect organizations to be diligent in ensuring that these costs are justified and controlled.

IT strategy also includes planning for technology obsolescence. Technology that is inadequate for the enterprise or becomes obsolete too soon is a growing concern. This has an adverse effect on productivity, cost efficiency as well as on security. Technology is changing at a rapid pace, and unless organizations constantly upgrade their IT infrastructure, their business will suffer.

The responsibility of the CEO involves adopting a risk control and governance framework, embedding responsibilities for risk management in the organization and monitoring IT risks and accepting residual IT risks.

The responsibility of assessing risks and mitigating them to ensure that they are transparent to the stakeholders, implementing an IT control framework, and ensuring that roles critical for managing IT risks are appropriately defined and staffed lies with the CIO.

Ultimately, individuals across the organizational hierarchy need to be aware of their responsibilities towards an effective IT risk management programme. Building a fence around IT risk to separate it from the rest of your organizational activity will not work because the alignment of your IT strategy to your business strategy will underline the success and even the survival of your organization.

In addition, the Department of Company Affairs, Government of India, constituted a nine-member committee under the chairmanship of Mr. Naresh Chandra, former Indian ambassador to the U.S., to examine various corporate governance issues. The committee's recommendations are now mandatory.

The corporate governance philosophy is based on the following principles:

1. Satisfy the spirit of the law and not just the letter of the law. Corporate governance standards should go beyond the law.
2. Be transparent and maintain a high degree of disclosure levels. When in doubt, disclose.
3. Make a clear distinction between personal conveniences and corporate resources.
4. Communicate externally, in a truthful manner, about how the company is run internally.
5. Comply with the laws in all the countries in which the company operates.
6. Have a simple and transparent corporate structure driven solely by business needs.
7. Management is the trustee of the shareholders' capital and not the owner.

Ministry of Company Affairs (MCA-21 Portal)

February 18, 2006 will go down as a landmark day in the history of corporate governance in India. On this day, the MCA-21 project portal (www.mca21.gov.in) was launched in Coimbatore. This project of the Ministry of Company Affairs (MCA) is expected to provide 21st century services to business, government and the citizens of India, hence the name.

This portal will be the entry point for online registration, filing of returns, reporting financial results and requests for permissions by businesses, their number has grown from 30,000-plus companies in 1956, when the ministry was formed, to 6, 50,000 today. It will also be a tool for the public to report investor grievances. It will help the government to exercise control on erring corporations who delay or deny information. In fact, when fully operational, MCA-21 will usher in a new phase in the history of corporate governance in India.

Online processing itself imaginatively uses the 'forms' feature of Adobe PDF file, which permits data filling without modifying the form itself; downloadable paper-based forms that can be filled offline may also be used. Companies who want to transact online have to take digital certificates so that authenticity and accountability are maintained, in addition to security. The Indian government has already put in place the necessary Controller of Certification Authority (CCA) (www.cca.gov.in). Several Certification Authorities have been licensed by CCA. The legislation to allow e-filing was also provided recently, through an ordinance in early 2006.

Salient Features of the MCA-21

- Corporations, professionals and the public at large will no longer need to visit the Registrar of Company offices and would be able to interact with the Ministry using the MCA-21 portal from their offices or home or by going to the facilitation centers, which have been set-up.
- The users will have multiple options to make payments in the online mode either through credit cards or the Internet banking facility. Besides this, the traditional payment through demand draft would be accepted against a system-generated challan at more than 200 bank branches across the country.
- The programme also introduces the concept of Director Identification Number (DIN), which is a unique and lifetime identification number being issued to all current and prospective directors. It is mandatory for all directors who wish to interact with the ministry in future to acquire a DIN.
- The system would also enable the stakeholder to track the service request through a Service Request Number (SRN).
- The MCA-21 project will also facilitate electronic submission of forms, which require a unique Digital Signature Certificate (DSC). It is also mandatory for all the stakeholders who would interact with the ministry to have a DSC, since without that, it would not be possible to file the returns and other statutory compliance related filing.

The Goals of "MCA-21" are

- Business facilitated to register a company and file statutory documents quickly and easily.
- Public to get easy access to relevant records.

- Professionals to be able to offer efficient services to their client companies.
- Financial Institutions to find registration and verification of charges easy.
- MCA to ensure proactive and effective compliance of relevant laws and corporate governance.
- Employees enabled to deliver better services.

Conclusion

The corporate governance is finding new definitions and widening day after day with new practices with the aid of Information Technology. The project MCA-21 is an evident in this respect. Corporate Governance and I.T. are opening new horizons for use by the public and needy organizations leading to greater transparency, which obviously improve the confidence of citizens at large especially various type of tax systems like Income tax, value added tax etc. This, not only solidify revenue collection system but also inevitable to distribute the same in a transparent method, resulting in curbing down the corruption practices.

REFERENCES

1. *Financial Express*, February 16, 2006.
2. *The Economic Times*, February 4, 2006.
3. www.mca21.gov.in
4. Charkham, Jonathan (1994), "Keeping Good Company: A Study of Corporate Governance in Five Countries"; Oxford: Clarendon Press.
5. "Corporate Governance" by P.P. Arya; B.B.Tandon; A.K.Vashisht, Deep and Deep Publications Pvt. Ltd., 2003.

15

Corporate Governance—A Conceptual Framework

M. S. R. Sesha Giri and Dr. B. Madhukar

The Origin

Towards the end of twentieth century rapid growth of industrialization led to a crucial debate over the separation of ownership control and management of the organizations. Thus in the mid 1920s A.Berle and G.Means had propounded a theory named "The modern corporation and private property", which can be said as the oldest inevitable source for today's so-called corporate governance. But it has been ignored all the way in latter years. Again towards the end of 1980s the mis-governance which had been taken place in various organizations throughout the world; especially in US and UK; has led the vision of various governments and the investors towards the importance of corporate governance. In this concern; besides the separation of ownership and control, factors effecting are responsible governance in the politics and among various stakeholders in respective nations; has been argued by Mark Roe in his book which has been titled "Strong Managers Weak Owners: The Political Role of American Corporate Finance." In 1991 a committee was set-up in UK named "Cadbury Committee" under the chairmanship of Sir Adrian Cadbury which said as the base provider for the present day's scenario of corporate governance. In the recent days there has been increasing contribution from many of the modern authors towards better development and implementation of Corporate Governance.

Definition

It can be said that no definition is concrete related to corporate governance; still precise of the available is "Corporate Governance is the system by which companies are directed and controlled" (Performance and Accountability).

Objective

The laws in any country provide guidelines on "What a board should not do rather than what it should do." It does not suggest the system, structures and procedures that would lead to more objective and well informed set of corporate decisions that are likely to be free from self interest. In this view the ultimate objective of corporate Governance can be said as "Corporate Governance system encompasses the structural and behavioural issues of the corporate board as to how it should respond to its shareholders, financiers, government and employees—"the stakeholders". In a broader sense, it means how the corporate board responds to regulatory and environmental aspects.

Simply,

1. Enhancement of shareholders value, keeping in view the interests of other stakeholders.
2. Preservation and the greater practicable enhancement over time of their shareholder's investment.
3. Check on transparency, accountability and reporting system.

Various Systems/Models

We can classify various systems of the corporate governance by examining certain factors such as the composition of board of directors, their autonomy and the separation of management part from the ownership part, orientations of the investors and the protection provided by the law. Accordingly the systems existing in the developed economies can be discussed as below:

1. *Anglo-American model:* Even though there are variations in the compositions of boards, where an average American board consists of 80 per cent of outside directors. In USA, the roles of executive and non-executive directors are not separated, whereas, in UK since the boards are dominated by insiders (60%). Public companies have non-executive chairman of the boards, and he is expected to put check on the activities of the management.

   The Anglo-American institutions operate in regulated environment that discourages economic concentration and encourages free competition. The business environment in these countries facilitates self-reliance and individual wealth creation. Here the investors own stocks in companies either directly or through institutional investors. These institutions are banks, Mutual Funds, Pension Funds, insurance companies etc. The public corporations are truly owned by public. Salient features of this model are:

Ownership of Company

The ownership of the companies is more or less equally divided between individual shareholders and institutional shareholders. Though the combined holding of institutional shareholders is often more than 50 per cent, rarely does a single institutional investor have more than 10 per cent stake in a company.

1. *Management of company:* Companies are typically run by professional managers who have negligible ownership stakes. There is a fairly clear separation of ownership and management. Managers enjoy substantial freedom in running the companies and the typical chief executive officer considers himself as wielding complete control.
2. *Independence of directors:* Though in theory the management is supposed to be chosen by the directors, in practice, often it is the other way. Hence, directors are rarely independent of management.
3. *Myopic outlook:* [Short-term orientation of investors.] Most of the institutional investors are reluctant activists. They view themselves as portfolio investors interested in investing in a broadly diversified portfolio of liquid securities. The high churning ratio of these investors suggests that they have a short-term orientation. If they are not satisfied with a company's performance, they simply sell its securities in the market. The myopic outlook of institutional investors builds pressure on management to report good earnings performance in short-run.
4. *Role of institutional investors:* Most of the institutional investors seem to have neither the inclination nor the ability to monitor companies effectively, a small, and perhaps growing, number of institutional investors a more active role in corporate governance. We may classify them into two categories:

(i) Institutional investors investing in few companies and actively and monitoring them.

(ii) Institutional investors who pursue "index strategy".

5. *Adequate protection to the small investor*: The disclosure norms are comprehensive, the rules against insider trading tight, and the penalties for price manipulation stiff. These measures provide adequate protection to the small investor and promote general market liquidity. Incidentally, they also discourage large investors from taking an active role in corporate governance.
6. *Threat of takeovers:* There is fairly active market for corporate control that provides a credible threat of takeover to consistent under performers. Hostile deals, along with leverage buy-outs and other transactions in corporate control, enriched shareholders. The significant hostile takeover activity laments the recent political and legal reaction against takeovers.
7. *Conclusion:* The goal of corporate governance in this model can be said as 'the creation and enhancement of shareholders' wealth'. This model, because of the important role of chief executive officer, active capital markets, short-term , and credible take over threats can be named as "high tension".

German and Japanese Model

The composition of a Japanese board is same as that of the Anglo American countries which could be said as a unitary board, where as in Germany the boards are, in compliance with law are "two-tiered". They are the management board which is composed of executive directors who look after day-to-day corporate activities, and the other supervision board, is composed of non-executive directors, who cannot be a member of management board, and are equally nominated by the owners and employees. The law insists that the chairmanship of these boards should always be held by two different individuals. And a power of veto is given to the management board chairman in case of tie.

The corporations in these countries aim at collective welfare. The Germans are less wary of concentration of economic power and favour cooperative approach to corporate governance. They involve government, creditors and labour to certain extent in corporate decision-making. Public ownership is less dispersed than US and UK. Banks and insurance companies are the major institutional investors. Banks mostly holds the custody of voting power of individuals' shares. They generally hold on their stakes for a much longer time to promote collective welfare. In Japan, a corporate is considered as a family member. Corporations are expected to treat stakeholders as extended family members by promoting their long-term interest. Market forces play only subordinate role and the interests of the government and business are closely aligned to each other. Here the corporations are largely owners' controlled in contrast with that of the Anglo-American ones. The ownership is characterized by an extensive network of cross-holding that generally include banks, suppliers, sub-contractors and customers. These shareholders are abided by a strong tacit mutual agreement of not selling the shares that are held reciprocally and support each other's business and commercial activities. Important features of this model are:

(a) *Equity capital:* Banks and financial institutions have substantial stake in the equity capital of companies, cross-holdings among groups of firms is common in Japan.

(b) *Long-term orientation of institutions investors:* Institutional investors in these countries view themselves as long-term investors. They play fairly active role in management. In general, the long-term commitment of institution and the close monitoring provided by them seem to have helped companies immensely.

(c) *Imparity in the efficiency of the capital market:* Here the disclosure norms are not very stringent, checks on insider trading are not very comprehensive and effective, and the emphasis on liquidity is not high. All this tends towards imparity in efficiency of the capital markets.

(d) *Rare takeovers:* There is hardly any market for corporate control in these countries. Hence takeovers are very rare.

(e) *Conclusion:* Because of the access to vast information system through banks, long-terms of investors, infrequent mergers and acquisitions, limited role of capital market this model can be said as "Networked system".

Corporate Governance in Indian Scenario

Corporate Governance in India has gained momentum during late 90s. (This is because of liberalization from 1991).The system of governance operates in an administered environment. Prior to liberalization also few Companies used to practice in India. The new archetype of corporate governance is in tune with the changing times, which demands high degree of accountability to its shareholders and customers, economic liberalization and deregulation of industry and business in India. The Cadbury Committee Report has also given impetus to the debate on corporate governance in our country.

A Committee on Corporate Governance was set-up on May 7 1999, by the SEBI under the Chairmanship of Shri Kumar Mangalam Birla, to raise the standards of Corporate Governance in India and the committee submitted its report during February, 2000.

The Committee acknowledged that financial report and disclosure which are also related to the accounting policies of a company and the practicing accounting norms and auditing ways, are the main indicators of Corporate Governance.

Key factors of corporate governance related to finance are:

- Summarizing accounts of auxiliaries.
- Separate accounting for different kinds of business organized by one company.
- Disclosure and treatment of related party transactions.
- Treatment of deferred taxation.

Nothing will happen if we simply frame corporate governance rules and policies, but we need to implement the same. Even now, some companies are following existing models, without the subsistence of formal guidelines in this subject. Structures and rules are important because they provide a framework which will encourage and enforce good governance. But these alone cannot raise the standards of corporate governance. What counts is, the way in which these are put to use. The Committee has framed the codes of Corporate Governance and has also suggested the implementation of the code through stock exchange similar to that of UK.

For example, companies quoted on the London and Toronto Stock Exchanges formally need not follow the recommendations of their respective national codes. However, they must disclose whether they follow the recommendations in those documents or not. Otherwise they should provide explanations concerning divergent practices. Such disclosure requirements exert a significant pressure on listed companies for compliance.

It has identified three vital aspects relating to the corporate governance:

(i) Shareholders,

(ii) Board of Directors, and

(iii) Management.

(SEBI Clause 49) insists appointment of Independent Directors by all listed companies keeping in view the interests of the shareholders.

Reasons for Poor Governance in India

1. In India most of the corporates are either family business units or government owned. Since a large proportion of shares held by the above it is difficult to bring changes in the existing system.
2. In family oriented business units, the founders may be reluctant to grant authority to employed directors.
3. In India policy makers are different from the one who implement, which may result in to ineffective governance.
4. Time lags in Public sector units in India may cause delay in implementing any policies.
5. In India Skepticism is more prevalent among owners of business units in the fear of leakage of vital information of the company.
6. The Indian corporate sector, as such, suffering from lack of independent directors who can deliver the best.
7. In Global context MNCs pay its directors a hefty amount, whereas it is very less in our country.

Some Guidelines to Make Corporate Governance More Effective

1. In order to achieve good corporate governance, the commitment and capability of outside directors and the hesitation

of nominated directors to discuss strategic issues with the board; plays a vital role. This resulted into bringing activism among institutional investors or individual investors which initiated various board reforms across the countries.

2. Prepare a well defined organization structure with no ambiguity of roles at each level.
3. There must be an alignment in the interest of both the management and the owners. It helps in mitigating the agency costs (Alignment of interest).
4. Contrary to the above there must be a real possibility of extricate the managers if they under perform (Contestability).
5. Have a Board with directors from within and outside the company, who have no business or personal links with largest shareholders or with promoters (Include Non-executives as directors).
6. Broaden the mandate of the board so that it can advise and add value to the company's strategic and tactical moves.
7. Appoint various committees like audit, remuneration, compliance, stock options, succession planning, employee responsibility and environmental responsibility and also review each committee's performance at regular intervals.
8. Draw up and ensure compliance with pre-determined parameters as far as company's financial performance.
9. To integrate Indian economy with world economy.
10. The degree of accountability the corporate board shows towards its stockholders is the benchmark for the corporate governance of high standards. Profits have no relation with the kind of corporate governance model.

Conclusion

Since the Indian economy is steadily growing at a rate of 7-8 per cent per annum, most of the foreign investors are showing keen interest for investment in our country. They are also insisting upon implementation of good (corporate) governance.

Hence, it is very much necessary for the Indian Government to pay utmost attention on effective implementation of principles of corporate governance.

BIBLIOGRAPHY

1. N. Gopalaswamy, *Corporate Governance—The New Paradigm,* Wheeler Publishing, A Division of A.H. Wheeler & Co., Ltd., New Delhi, 1998.
2. Indian Banks Association, Indian Banking Book, Mumbai, 2003.
3. Vepakesam, "Corporate Governance", Reserve Bank of India Bulletin, January 2000, pp. 21-43.
4. http/www.google.com
5. http/www.dogpile.com
6. http/www.ungoogle.com
7. Devi Singh and Subhash Garg, Excel Books, first edition, New Delhi, 2001, "Corporate Governance".
8. Charted Financial Analyst (old issues), ICFAI Press.
9. Media release, *The Hindu,* Business line.
10. SEBI Guidelines (Clause 49).

16

Impact of Right to Information Act on Corporate Governance

Mr. K. Visweswara Rao and Mr. N. Siva Rama Krishna

Corporate governance is concerned with the formulation of long-term objectives and plans, the proper management structure to achieve them. And at the same time, it entails making sure that the structure functions to maintain the corporation's identity and responsibility to its various constituencies. The importance that has been attached to corporate governance these days is mainly due to two factors. First, in the post-liberlisation era, the intervention of government in either deciding prices or supply of essential commodities has decreased a lot. Earlier government used to restrict the fluctutations in prices of some essential commodities and its intervention was high in ensuring continuous supply. Now, everything is left to market forces. Nowadays, competition is the one which is going to decide the market dynamics of a commodity. Second factor is increased world trade which led to the formulation of regulatory organizations like WTO, OECD etc., who established certain rules that companies have to follow in their governing procedure.

One more factor of concern is Sensex. It has touched the ever highest 10,000 mark, which is the result of increased confidence of both domestic and foreign institutional investors in stock market. An average Indian is generally of conservative nature and he does not like to take high risk with his investments. That is why the growth of capital market in India was at a very low ebb till recent times. But with the advent of the Business Process Outsourcing (BPO) and India's cost effective manpower, Indian youth got good employment opportunities and an average Indian is left with good amount of purchasing power. With the increased surplus income and decreased interest rates on bank deposits even common people are able to direct their investments into stock market with the desire of getting higher returns. This is a good sign for Indian capital market.

To increase the confidence of investors and to increase their wealth making opportunities corporates need to concentrate on effective governing procedure. When investments take place in emerging markets in the form of FIIs the investors want to be sure that not only are the capital markets or enterprises with which they are investing, run competently but they also have good corporate governance.

How to define good corporate governance or how to say decisions that were taken by management are within the legal framework or not? To decide this there are three-way tests for ethics prescribed by Normal Vincent Peale and Kenneth Blanchard in their book "Power of Ethical Management". The three-point test is:

(a) Is the decision you are taking legal? If it is not legal it is not ethical.

(b) Is the decision you are taking fair? In other words it should be win-win situation for both the parties entering into an agreement or if it is a general policy or a multi-level agreement, there should be equal risk and reward for all concerned. If it is not fair then the decision is not ethical.

(c) The third decision what can be called the Eleventh Commandment test. It is said by cynics that there are Ten Commandments in the Bible but there is Eleventh Commandment which is hidden. You can violate all the ten commandments but thou shall not be found out. If the decision you are taking is such that if it is known in the public through the media, will you feel ashamed? If you are feeling ashamed then it is not an ethical decision. The embarrassment caused by the Tehelka.com expose was because those figuring in the tapes were found guilty of violating the Eleventh Commandment.

Corporate governance represents the value framework, the ethical framework and the moral framework under which business decisions are taken. The investors want to be sure that not only their capital handled effectively but also the decisions that were taken are within the moral and legal framework. Corporate governance therefore calls for two factors.

(a) Transparency in decision-making.

(b) Accountability to fix the responsibilities to individuals in the organization whether decisions taken or not taken and for safeguarding the interests of the shareholders.

Corporate governance depends upon two more factors. The first is the commitment of the management for the principle of integrity and transparency in business operations. The second is legal and administrative framework created by the government. Ultimately, the corporate governance is the net result of individual sense of values, the values held in society or part of a society like professional bodies or business associations and finally the system of public governance.

Implementation of corporate governance has depended upon laying down explicit codes, which enterprises and the organization are supposed to observe. The Cadbury's code in U.K. was the starting point. London Stock Exchange formed this committee to evolve a code of good corporate governance in 1991 and it became foundation for committees to come. In India itself we have the Kumara Mangalam Birla Code as a result of the committee headed by him at the behest of SEBI. Earlier we had the CII coming up with the code for corporate governance recommended by the committee headed by Sri Rahul Bajaj. The codes however can only be a guideline. Ultimately effective corporate governance depends upon the commitment of the people in the organization. If the public governance is weak we cannot have good corporate governance because corporate governance is also dependent on legal and administrative framework. Here are some of the examples of ineffective corporate governance, which in turn reflects the lack of effectiveness in legal and administration framework.

Enron

Enron Corporation is a typical multinational company - dishonest, unscrupulous, greedy, and downright corrupt. It has gone bankrupt, and some of its officers are being hauled before the Congress and the Senate. The corporation has cheated the public, its own shareholders and employees and has been up to all kinds of skullduggery. Enron filed for bankruptcy in December 2001 as it was unable to repay its huge debts. There are also several other charges against the company and its officials. Its books have been cooked over the last few years and have no relation with the actual state of affairs. It has been bribing politicians in Washington and elsewhere and so far spent over $ 6 billion in what are known as contributions to election funds but are no different from bribes. And its officers have made millions by selling their shares before the company went bankrupt, though it would not permit its employees to do so. The employees have lost their life's savings while most senior officers have become millionaires ten times over. How can such a thing happen in a country like America, where there are so many regulators who keep a watch over financial deal? Actually, America is not all that clean when it comes to corporates. The business of the United States is business, they used to say. Now businessmen themselves are ruling the country. George W Bush is a businessman. His vice-president Dick Cheney is a businessman. His Ex-Defense secretary, Donald Rumsfeld, is a businessman. Even his Defense Secretary, Condoleeza Rice, used to be a director on the board of an oil company. In fact, all these people are connected with petroleum industry, and so was Enron.

The year before it collapsed, it had posted sales of nearly 100 billion dollars, or about Rs. 500,000 crore, which made it the seventh biggest company in the US. But these figures were bogus and so were its profits. What the company did was to float several smaller companies which, however, remained outside its balance-sheet. These companies gambled heavily on oil and gas futures and made huge profits. The profits and sales went through Enron's accounts, but not the debts.The debts were actually guaranteed by Enron.Net result was that Wall Street was made to believe that Enron was a hugely profitable company, growing faster than anybody had imagined. This is how its scrip went up to $90 last year, from as low as $10 four years before. Enron's Dabhol Power Company was also a fraudulent affair..Elntoh is supposed to have spent $3 billion on the project.It turns out that this may not be true.Most people say that the actual amount may have been no more than $2 billion. This means that Enron has tried a fast one on us, which is precisely what it has done in the US.

The modus operandi seems to be also the same. In the US, Enron contributed handsomely to the election funds of politicians. Here it bribed our politicians, right and left which is precisely why our politicians, which include governments in Maharashtra as well as Delhi, have kept quiet so far.The Dabhol crisis has been brewing for the last one year, may be longer, but our politicians have been behaving as if it has nothing to do with it. In fact, the power ministry in Delhi is on record saying that the problem with Dabhol has to be sorted out between Enron and the State Government of Maharashtra, and the Centre does not come into the picture. The ministry is wrong. It was after all the Central Cabinet that had given sovereign guarantees to Enron, which means that ultimately the ball is in its court.

Dabhol has an equity of $1,200 million and a debt of $1,800 million.Enron can always go back to the Centre for redeeming this debt which it would be bound to do so, because of its guarantee.

Actually, Dabhol Power Company went bust because the State Government of Maharashtra refused to purchase its excessively costly power. The Government of Maharashtra is the only government to stand up to Enron's bullying. The tariff was the result of complicity between Enron and the politicians of Maharashtra and Delhi, who underwrote the proposals and received huge bribes totalling over $200 billion or about Rs. 800 crore (out of the total project cost of Rs.12,000 crore).

Although at least half the money invested in Dabhol is public money since the bulk of the debt is provided by the Indian financial institutions, there has been no move on the part of the Central Government to intervene in the matter. The political class in India is not only just incompetent and corrupt but it is also gutless. While the Enron saga has been going on for the last five or six weeks since the company went bankrupt, the Central Government is behaving as if it was none of its business. I am also surprised that the Maharashtra governrment is also silent as if paralysed by the goings on. This is actually the time for the governrnent, in conjunction with the Centre, to take the matter to court, just as the matter is now with the Justice Department in Washington. There are reports that Enron has been removing sensitive materials from Dabhol without taking permission from the government. This is a serious matter that calls for immediate government action.

The whole project is a case of a nexus between the political class and the business class, each feeding on the other. The commission should also find out who was responsible for okaying the so-called power purchase agreement under which the state electricity board is under compulsion to purchase power at exorbitant rates that can go up to Rs. 12 a unit, depending on dollar-rupee parity.

UTI

The amount robbed through the UTI scam intails thousands of crores—the bulk of which belongs to small investors who have put their life-savings into this scheme.The Unit Trust of India is the largest mutual fund in the country created in 1964 through an act of Parliament. Mutual Funds are financal institutions that invest people's money in various schemes, giving a gauranteed return to the investor. The UTI (of which the US-64 scheme is the largest) was set-up specifically to channel small savings of citizens into investments giving relatively large returns/interest. The US-64 scheme has 2 crore investors, the bulk of whom are small savers, retired people, widows and pensioners. Besides the US-64, UTI runs 87 other schemes giving investors various options. But the US-64 has been most popular, giving returns as high as 18 per cent in 1993 and 1994.

Liberalisation of the economy immediately led to the liberalisation of the UTI, throwing it to the mercy of the stock market. In 1992, itself the US-64 scheme was changed from a debt-based fund to one linked to equity. In 1992 only 28 per cent of its fund was in equity; today it is over 70 per cent. Further liberalisation was pushed by Chidambram, as the finance minister of the UF Government, who, in 1997, removed all government nominees from the board of the UTI. Besides, the US-64 does not come under SEBI regulations, its investment details are kept secret (ever depositors cannot know where their funds are being parked) and the chairman has arbitrary powers to personally decide an investment upto a huge Rs. 40 crore. Such 'liberalisation' is tailor-made for frauds. Not surprisingly, within one year of Chidambram's liberalisation, in 1998, the UTI crashed, and the new BJP-led government organised a large Rs. 3,500 crore bail-out to prevent default.

Huge amount of UTI funds were channeled into the infamous K-10 list of Ketan Parekh stock, such as Himachal Futuristic, Zee Telefilms, Global Tele, DSQ, etc. They continued to buy these shares even when their market value began to crash in mid-2000, in order to prop up the share values of these stocks. The Trust saw its Rs. 30,000 portfolio (value of stocks) lose half its value within a year since February, 2000.

To take just one example on how they operated: In August 2000, much after the software stocks had begun to crash, the UTI bought Rs. 34 crore worth of shares in Cyberspace Infosys Ltd at the huge price of Rs. 930 per share. Today the shares have no value and its Lucknow based promoters, the Johari Group, are in jail. But, what is astounding is that it was none other than India's prime minister, Vajpayee, who, as late as January 31,2001, laid the foundation stone for the Software Technology Park (STP) in Luknow, promoted by this group. (Incidentally the UP Government had a 26 per cent share in this STP). Coincidentally, in the four days when it reversed its earlier decision and subscribed to 3.45 lakh shares of Cyberspace, (SubramanyaJ)} had rung up N.K. Singh (then secretary in the PMO) at least 4 times. It does not take much imagination to link the purchases in Cyberspace with Vajpayee. Similar were the investments in DSQ Software, HFCL, Sriram Multitech and others.

Besides, the UTI also invested in junk bonds like Pritish Nandy Communications (Rs. 1.5 crore), Jain Studios (Rs. 5 crores), Sanjay Khan's Numero Uno International (Rs. 7.5 crores), Malavika Spindles (Rs. 188 crore) etc. This amounted to nothing but handing over people's money (investments) to the rich all powerful. Thereby thousands of crores were siphoned off to big business and prominent individuals, with the chairman, bureaucrats and politicians taking their cuts.

All these kinds of scams or frauds are mainly due unscrupulous governing procedure which entails lack of transparency. There is a strong relationship between democracy and information. It has been said that right to information is foundation for democracy.

On 12th October, 2005, the UPA brought Right to Information Act into the application.

Right to information means the right of access to information relating to affairs of the state or public bodies by means of obtaining certified copies of document. As we have already seen that for effective corporate governance besides the commitment of management for integrity, strong legal and administrative framework is also very much essential. Keeping this in view, Right to Information would be a very strong weapon for a common man to know information regarding the PDS, government actions, details of projects, state of PSUs etc.

There are lots of queries regarding RTI that will it be able to open all cupboards of vital information, private and public. Besides unraveling skeletons in government cupboards, newshounds constantly expose corruption in the corporate sector and its cost and consequences for the investor public. However, corporate information is not as readily available for newsmen or the public as information they could demand from public to state agencies after the passage of the Right to Information Bill.

REFERENCES

1. Vickypedia.com.
2. Google.com.
3. Dogpiles.com.
4. hindu.com.
5. indiainfoline.com.

17

Corporate Governance in India

Dr. B. Madhukar and Smt. P. V. Mohini

In the early half of 20th century, Indian corporates were largely ruled under the British dominance and managing framework. The Companies Act, 1956, is also largely based on the provisions of English law. This made Indian corporates to follow the British corporate Governance system. Indian Corporate Governance system follows the pattern of Anglo-American model,with the primary aim of the corporate to look after the interests of shareholders. The ownership dispersion has been specially encouraged by Corporate Laws and Regulations, Financial Institutions, Corporate bodies and public have been largely the major owners of the Indian corporates. The boards are basically unitary as those of the British ones. There is no legal provision in Indian company law to nominate non-executive director on board. Even though few companies are electing non-executive directors, it can be said that it is for other commercial benefits rather than for better Corporate Governance. The law does not specifically separate the executive and non-executive component of the board and therefore, by and large, Indian Boards are acting in a very cozy relationship with the executive management and offers no check against the corporate action of the management prejudicial to shareholders and other stakeholders. Generally the Indian Institutional Investors have not been observed proactive to enhance the value for company and its shareholders or prevented the management from taking less optimal decisions or following unacceptable or unethical corporate practices. With respect to this situation we can classify the corporate governance systems in India into two types. They are:

- ***Corporate Governance System in Private Sector:*** Important features of the system are:
  - *Categories of shareholders:* There are three broad categories of shareholders, namely, (1) Promoters, (2) Financial Institutions, and (3) Individual Investors. On an average all the three categories are more or less equally important, though there are large variations across the companies.
  - *Majority rule voting system:* For electing the Directors, the majority rule voting system is typically followed.
  - *Types of board of directors:* Company Boards generally comprise three types of Directors. (1) Promoter Directors, (2) Professional Directors, (3) Institutionally-Nominated Directors. Usually promoter directors belong to promoter group. Professional directors are persons of eminence who are invited by the promoters mainly on the basis of favourable personal equations and, the institutionally-nominated directors are either senior executives of the institutions or persons of repute. While, the professional directors who are invited by the promoters are found to be strong, the institutionally-nominated directors are weak in terms of incentives, candid behaviour and scarifying their forthrightness at the altar of courtesy and politeness. These tendencies are further strengthened by the dynamics of the small groups, wherein the promoter-directors pay special attention to cultivate others.
  - *Management by chromosomes:* Institutional Investors in general, have been supportive of promoters. They seem to implicitly subscribe to the principle which can be referred as "Management by Chromosomes". They interfere only when a crisis develop or when there is a clear evidence of malafide behaviour on the part of management, or when there is a directive to them from the Government. Institutional-Nominees on company boards hardly have any incentive to monitor the behaviour and performance of management seriously.
  - *Scattered and ill-organised individual shareholders:* Individual shareholders have, by and large, been

benign, tolerant and ignorant. Though there are some knowledgeable shareholders who raise sensible querries in the Annual General Meetings, they are not able to accomplish much, because the management enjoys an informal advantage and know how to retain the support of most of the shareholders by offering few sops here and there, and portraying a glowing picture that enthuses them. Scattered and ill-organised, individual shareholders are not in a position to play a meaningful role in electing directors. Further the majority rule voting system prevents even a well organised substantial minority to have any say in the election of Board of Directors.

— *Greater entrepreneurial vigour of business houses:* Family managed companies in general, seem to display greater entrepreneurial vigour, act more proactively and exercise strict control. However, the virtually unchallenged control of family provides a lot of scope for self-dealing and facilitates personal enrichment at the expense of company. The degree to which these aberrations may occur depends on the level of integrity of the controlling family.

— *Slow reactiveness of professionally managed companies:* These companies, in general, react somewhat slowly towards the new opportunities and challenges put greater emphasis on systems, favour the interest of incumbent management over that of the shareholders, and set relatively easy performance standards.

— *Conclusion:* Due to the firm hold of the promoters over the companies managed by them and the disinclination or inability of others to challenge them, this system may be characterised as the *Entrenched System*.

■ ***Corporate Governance System in Public Sector:*** Important features of the system:

— *Ownership equity shares:* The equity shares are wholly or substantially owned by the Government. Technically, the shares of the Central Public Sector Undertakings are held in the name of the President of India.

— *Categories of board of directors:* There are three categories of Board of Directors in this system (1) Functional Directors, (2) Government Directors, (3) Outside Directors. The Functional Directors are the full-time employees of the concerned Public Sector undertaking, Government Directors are Bureaucrats from the controlling administrative ministry.

— *Potential and bureaucratic influence:* There is, in general, a good deal of political and bureaucratic influence over the management of public sector undertakings, which often substantially erodes the autonomy of the Management.

— *Excessive emphasis on observing rules, regulations and guidelines:* PSUs are constrained by various regulations and administrative guidelines. They are also subjected to the CAG audit and accountability to the Parliament. In this concern efficiency and performance are often sacrificed at the altar of propriety.

— *Short tenure of CEOs:* Chief Executives of PSUs have short tenures often one to three years. It is rare to find a CEO to hold the affairs for more than five years. During such a short tenure, coupled with limited freedom, leads to myopic outlook. It is rare to find a visionary leader guiding the destiny of a PSU with a long planning horizon. Most of the CEOs seem to be concerned with fulfilled short-term targets emanating from the MoUs.

— *Weak accountability:* In general, performance standards are soft, compensation levels low, incentives for performance are poor, and 'real' accountability weak.

— *Conclusion:* The Myopic view of key players such as politicians, bureaucrats and Managers, this system may be characterised as the *'Transient System'*.

For Better Corporate Governance

Confederation of Indian Industry had constituted a National Task Force on corporate governance. This task force has suggested the Indian Corporate Board to comply the following recommendations in order to move gradually towards the International standards of Corporate Governance:

- The non-executive directors have to play an important role in maximizing long-term shareholder value, by becoming active participants in boards, having clearly defined responsibilities with in the board and knowing how to read Balance Sheet, Profit and Loss account, Cash Flow Statements and Financial Ratios and have some knowledge of various Company laws.
- The following issues require closer scrutiny of corporate actions by an independent party.
  - Financial Performance of the company
  - Payment of Institutional, Government and Statutory dues
  - Inter-corporate investment and deposits
  - Investment in, and loans to subsidiaries
  - Award of contracts for works
  - Mergers and Acquisitions
  - Expansion and Diversification
  - Hiving off or transfer of company's divisions
  - Subsidisation and de-subsidisation
  - Changes in Articles of Association
  - Appointment of Chairman/Managing Director, reappointment or changes in terms of the same
  - Setting up of Joint-Ventures
  - Dividend and Bonus policies
  - Preferential issue of equity to promoter's group
  - Control over undue or extravagant expenditure
  - Raising of funds through rights issues/term loans/ debentures
  - Appointing committees such as audit/management committees and concurrent auditors.
- To secure better effort from non-executive directors, the company should pay a commission over and above the sitting fee for the use of professional inputs.

- While re-appointing members of the board, companies should give the attendance record of the concerned directors.
- Major Indian Stock Exchanges should gradually insist upon a compliance certificate, signed by CEO and the CFO.
- The Government must allow far greater funding to the corporate sector against the security of share and other papers.

According to *Cadbury Committee Report* the following are listed as *Code of Best Practices* for Corporate Governance:

- ***The Board of Directors***
  - The Board should meet regularly, retain full and effective control over the company and monitor the executive management.
  - There should be a clearly accepted division of responsibilities at the head of a company, which will ensure a balance of power and authority, such that no one individual had unfettered powers of decision. Where the chairman is also the chief executive, it is essential that there should be a strong and independent element on the board, with a recognized senior member.
  - The Board should include non-executive directors of sufficient caliber and number for their views to carry significant weight in the board's decisions.
  - The Board should include non-executive directors of sufficient reserved to it for making a decision to ensure that the direction and control of the company is firmly in its hands.
  - There should be an agreed procedure for directors in the furtherance of their duties to take independent professional advice if necessary, at the company's expense.
  - All directors should have access to the advice and services of the company secretary, who is responsible to the board for ensuring that board procedures are followed and that applicable rules and regulations are complied with. Any question of removal of the company secretary should be a matter for the board as a whole.

- ***Non-Executive Directors***
  - — Non-executive directors should bring an independent judgement to bear on issues of strategy, performance, resources, including key appointments, and standards of conduct.
  - — Non-executive directors should be appointed for specified terms and reappointment should not be automatic.
  - — Non-executive directors should be selected through a formal process and both the process and their appointment should be a matter for the board as a whole.
- ***Executive Directors***
  - — Directors' service contracts should not exceed three years without shareholders' approval.
  - — There should be full and clear disclosure of directors' total emoluments and those of the chairman and highest-paid UK director, including pension contributions and stock options. Separate figures should be given for salary and performance related elements and the basis on which performance is measured should be explained.
  - — Executive directors' pay should be subject to the recommendations of a remuneration committee made up wholly or mainly of non-executive directors.
- ***Reporting and Controls***
  - — It is boards' duty to present a balanced and understandable assessment of the company's position.
  - — The board should ensure that an objective and professional relationship is maintained with the auditors.
  - — The board should establish an audit committee of at least three non-executive directors with written terms of reference which deal clearly with its authority and duties.
  - — The directors should explain their responsibility for

preparing an accounts next to a statement by the auditors about their reporting responsibilities.

— The directors should report on the effectiveness of the company's system of internal control.

— The directors should report that the business is a going concern, with supporting assumptions or qualifications as necessary.

The Authors specially thank Mr. K. Sridhar, MBA Student for his Contribution to this Article.

18

National Seminar on Corporate Governance—For Building Global Competence

(A Summary of the Key-note Address)

Dr. B. Madhukar and Smt. P. V. Mohini

The Authors specially thank Mr. K.Sridhar, MBA Student for his Contribution to this Article.

In his key-note address, Dr. E.A.S. Sarma first referred to the process of globalisation that makes it imperative for the corporate sector to become competitive.

Critics of globalisation often tend to assume an ideological position, not appreciating the fact that, even in ancient times, our society not only functioned in a global environment but also took full advantage of the opportunities that such an environment provided. Taking cue from this, our strategy should be to convert the threats of globalisation into opportunities and make it an aggressive two-way process. For this, every segment of our economy needs to become competitive vis-à-vis the global bench-marks. One of the important segments in this is the area of corporate governance. Our corporates should recognize the importance of this and adapt themselves to the changes in the global environment that is constantly setting more and more stringent bench-marks.

Dr. Sarma then dealt with the concept of "governance" in general. He drew parallels between the government and the corporate systems. Both these forms reflect the well-known "agency" problem that arises whenever the primary stakeholder delegates day-to-day management control to an agent. More often than not, the oversight exercised by the primary stakeholder over the agent weakens and the agent tends to assume greater control than what is intended. In the government, the electorate that elects its representatives tends to lose control over the elected ones. In turn, the oversight that a legislature is expected to exercise over the political executive also diminishes. The processes at work within the corporate world are by and large similar.

It was as early as in 1932 that the Berle and Means study, "The Modern Corporation and Private Property" analysed the agency problem arising in the case of large corporations in USA. The study highlighted the concentration of economic power in the hands of such large corporations, the emergence of an influential class of professional managers and the threat this process is likely to pose to the democratic structures in that country. Despite these somewhat disconcerting findings, it took several decades for USA and others to realize the potential dangers involved in corporate governance.

The Cadbury Committee (1992) in UK carried out pioneering work on the norms that should apply to Corporate Governance as such. But, it was only when a series of corporate failures, starting with Enron, then Tyco, Worldcom etc. that severely jolted the confidence of the ordinary American investor, that the West chose to wake up and attempt an earnest introspection on the relationship between the primary stakeholder and the professional manager. Then followed a comprehensive discussion on the need for a code of best practices in Corporate Governance, as set out in the reports of the Blue Ribbon Committee (1996), the London Stock Exchange (1998), and so on.

With the rapidly expanding role of the large corporate bodies in India and in view of the need to prop up investor confidence in the financial intermediaries that channel domestic savings into productive investment in the country, SEBI set up the Kumaramangalam Birla Committee (1999) to develop best Corporate Governance norms that are appropriate for our own situation. Since the public sector occupied an important place in the economy, attempts were made to evolve similar norms for PSUs also.

By now, the norms of Corporate Governance are well understood. As far as the role and the responsibility of the Director of a company are concerned, suitable amendments have already been made to the Companies Act. With some of the Indian companies entering the global capital markets, attempts are already being made to adopt the stringent norms of Directors' liabilities and disclosure, as set out in Sarbanes-Oxley Act in USA. The need to induct independent Directors into the Boards has also been recognised, though the exact meaning of "independence" is still being debated. Systems of independent audit are in the process of being put in place. Similarly, there has been a great deal of discussion on situations of "conflict of interest" that often led to scams that hurt the investors.

It is a matter of serious concern that the small investor in India is still highly vulnerable to widespread occurrence of corporate mis-governance. Whether it is the Urban Cooperative Banks, or, NBFIs, there have been hundreds and hundreds of "vanishing" companies that function as fly-by-night operators, lure the gullible investors and disappear with their hard earned savings. While the regulators initiate proceedings against the culprits, there is hardly any case in which the victimized investor could get back his money. In most of these cases, lack of self-regulation and inadequate external regulation are the factors that contributed to such unfortunate developments. More often than not, there are glaring "conflict-of-interest" situations but the authorities tend to turn a blind eye to them.

For the Indian economy to be internally strong and externally competitive, there is urgent need for compliance with the best standards of corporate governance.

19

Corporate Governance in the New Millennium: A Review

V. V. Ajit Kumar

ABSTRACT

In this era of globalization the characteristics of successful companies depends on the ability of company to develop new technology and products which will generate wealth. Interest in corporate governance is a recent phenomenon. The phenomenon of suddenly appearing and equally sudden vanishing companies during the last 20 years coupled with the emergence of a new breed of shareholders like foreign investors, institutional investors and mutual funds and their demands for better governance practices has compelled the policy makers to think of the malpractices in corporate India.

The new millennium corporations shall change dramatically where distributed leadership, wider stakeholder base, environment protection, self-regulation, transparency and natural justice will dominate the scene rather than the traditional practices. In addition to financial capital, human capital and natural capital cultural capital will finally take its due place in fulfilling corporate governance norms Corporations will be transformed into a corporate community with self-regulation rather than internal control. Finally ethical issues are to be tackled on a war footing with the advent of new technology. Corporations must pledge to honour their obligation to society by becoming economic, intellectual and social assets to each nation and community in which they operate.

Corporate Governance is currently one of the major contentious issues confronted by business firms all over the world as investors are demanding good governance practices. It is a relatively new issue for the Indian industry. It has assumed greater importance in the context of what has happened to companies like Enron, Xerox, World Com. etc. Corporate governance can be traced back to early 1990's when a series of corporate mismanagement and failures were reported in UK which led to the formation of Adrian Cadbury committee who came out with their first document, laying the foundation to the present day format of the corporate governance.

This report was primarily based on the frauds perpetrated by some of the unscrupulous directors that were usurping stakeholders' money for their personal benefits. So the terms of reference of this committee were mainly on the financial aspects of the corporations and focused on the roles of the institutional investors, auditors and remuneration of the top executives along with some measures on internal controls. The Cadbury Committee's terms of reference were mainly restricted to issues related to accountability.

There is considerable difference of opinion on what corporate governance is all about. But one thing is very clear that corporate governance is nothing but a method of enhancing the corporate performance by monitoring and controlling the management performance through ensuring the accountability of the management to all stakeholders. Governance and accountability are two sides of the same coin and combination of these two factors should lead to both efficiency and marshalling of all the resources of the organization to increase not only shareholder value but the benefit of all stakeholders.

One of the major issues in this period (even in the early 21st century for that matter) was misappropriation of funds of the shareholders by so-called professional managers (read non-owner manager). Guth and Ginsberg suggested that corporate entrepreneurship concerns both innovation and restructuring of economic resources of the company, so good corporate governance should address the motivational and behavioural aspects of the managers. One method of motivation could be increasing the Ownership Stake of the Professional Managers (ESOP) but again the result may not be always positive as could be seen from the recent collapse of some major corporations in North America. Human greed and penchant for better and better life style had driven many CEO's to drive up the stock value by artificial means and reap the benefit by various modes of camouflaged insider trading.

Most of these cases emphasize the need for supervising and enforcing accountability of directors of corporations that have highly diffused and widely dispersed ownership mostly in cases of large corporations. Adrian Cadbury Report (1992) laid the framework of Corporate Governance.

The term transparency is no longer just a fashionable term but an imperative to be followed. Different types of stakeholders may require transparency in different degrees. For example, shareholders may require transparency in sales, costs and financial plans. Customers may be interested in the information regarding products, their quality etc., and the regulatory authorities may be concerned about safety rules, management ethics and environmental practices. Hence, Transparency can be defined as accessibility of information to the institutions stakeholders regarding matters that affect their interests. Therefore, transparency is needed in all the activities of the organization. The main drivers of transparency are rising levels of knowledge and business on the web, increase in communication technology, literacy rate of people etc.

Transparency is the only way to maintain trust among the people related to the organization. Therefore, it can be said that to sustain and achieve high performance in the knowledge economy, the firm has to develop a trustworthy environment, which in turn originates from transparency. Internet is a tool that is widely used to maintain transparency. In this context, internet not only consists of the World Wide Web, but also includes web logs, e-mail, mobile phone, laptop, wireless communication and several other similar devices that can be used as a medium of information. Today's generation is highly proficient in using these devices and when it enters the workforce it will prove to be a powerful factor for transparency as it demands authenticity and value from the corporations.

Characteristics of 21st Century Corporation

The following are likely to be the characteristics of a company in the mid-21st century.

- Business will be the key generator of wealth rather than state.
- The time-limited custodians of the company who will represent a wide range of section of the society will generate wealth.
- Competitive Advantage will be retained by innovation, constant to self-renewal and consistent learning for self-improvement.
- Clear understanding emerges where transparency and accountability will be the corner stones of success.
- Restraint from greed, ethical compliance and dedicated team

to succeed with knowledge management rather than intrigues and hypocritical work for beating the competition.

- Personality cult of late 20th century, in the form of economic leaders, will be replaced by distributed leadership of highly qualified technologists.
- In addition to financial capital, human capital and natural capital would play more decisive role to create wealth.
- Environmental protection will be one of the key priorities of the business.
- Trade Barriers will probably be a part of the history.
- Self-regulation, initiative and natural justice may replace box ticking.

Bases on these paradigms, new chapters in corporate governance will emerge. Late 20th century has seen emergence of many iconic leaders like Jack Welch, George Fischer (Kodak), Bill Gates, and George Soros and success of the organization is directly liked to these personalities. However, business process is too complicated even in the late 20th century to attribute success to only these cult figures. This can be related to the media type done to the movie stars and sports personalities. Warren Buffet had said correctly "People are voting for the artists rather than the painting."

Corporate Governance Redefined

There are many ways of looking at the definition or rather meaning of the word corporate governance; one of them is the "main purpose of it is to define a relationship between those who own it and those who manage it." This was probably adequate in 20th century but no more in the current century. The main purpose of it must be to maximize stakeholder value that is more diffused the current century than the one gone by. For far too long this value has been determined by only financial value. Now it has been realized that financial value may be a part of the total value chain. In the last century following values were completely ignored, they are:

- Natural Capital
- Human Capital
- Cultural Capital

The author admits it is very difficult to quantify these three values but it is certain that financial capital is a fraction of these values, which are going to play a very crucial role in this century. Progress in this century will be determined by how we utilize these resources for the benefit of the mankind; society and the planet we live in so that the corporations we preside over have long-term future. It has been realized that our progress will be defined more by Human, Natural and finally Cultural Capital rather than financial Capital.

Some companies have already put a value to their human capital and some more are in the process of doing so. Least a company can do is to value human beings in the right perspective and encourage them to add value to the organization. In this knowledge era, human capital is one, which will make the difference to the bottom as well as top line. Hence this resource has to be nurtured carefully to get the best return out of it. According to the World Bank's 1995 Wealth Index, the total valued of the human capital would be three times greater than all financial and manufactured capital manufactured capital reflected in the global balance sheet. Considering the growth of output of knowledge industry in the intervening period, the value may be four times in 2002.

So far as natural capital is concerned, it is still more difficult to quantify. It is estimated that the annual valued of biological/natural services that flow would be around $36 tr and considering a rate of return of 6 per cent the natural capital should be $600 tr. This compares well with gross world product of $39 tr. unless we take care of this natural capital like we do for our financial capital only catastrophe can stare at us.

Finally comes the cultural capital, which is the most important part of governance issues that is the core subject in this chapter. Any amount of legislation will not be able to bring into the desired effect unless there is a cultural change in the minds of the people who manage the business on behalf of the share/stakeholders. Good corporate governance is a source of competitive advantage and very critical to socio-economic progress of the society. Sharing of knowledge rather than sharing of physical or financial capital adds value to the society. Capital or physical assets can be used only in a particular way whereas knowledge can be used in many ways, as its is an intangible and fluid by nature; it can be transferred in a cost effective way and used in many ways depending on the type and nature of it. The best part of knowledge is, as Vishnu Sharma said in Panchatantra, that which does not diminish even if it is given away. Many applications of the same knowledge can generate wealth unlike financial and/or physical assets. Hence, knowledge management is one of major areas where governance and business ethics are going to be very critical.

Good Corporate governance is the key to efficiency in a competitive environment as it provides a cutting edge. It is necessary not just because it is good for the shareholders and other stakeholders it is essential because it is in the interest of the company itself in the present competitive environment. It is good for the shareholders because it is good for the company on which their future depends. If the quality of corporate governance is good, decision-making process should be transparent, consistent with the need to protect the competitive interests of the company as otherwise shareholders and other stakeholders in the enterprise would lose out. Corporate Governance will be an important instrument of investor protection.

20

Corporate Governance in the Era of LPG

K.V. V. Murali S. Rao, Kiran Kumar and S.T.G.R. Charyulu

"The governance of the corporation is now as important in the world economy as the government of countries."

James D. Wolfensohn, "A Battle for Corporate Honesty," The Economist: The World in 1999, p. 38.

Corporate Governance is the buzzword in today's Indian industry. A decade ago no one made any issue of it. The importance of governing organizations has been gaining momentum in our country, especially after liberalization. Every corporate is now looking at good deed from all the parties it dealt with like shareholders, society, government and stakeholders etc. Liberalization and Globalization of Indian economy in recent years has given a new dimension to the governance of corporate sector in the country. The old practices in-camera decisions and narrow outlook of the companies have given way to more transparent and professional process of decision-making in the corporate sector.

Corporate Governance

The processes and structure by which business and affairs of corporate sector is directed and managed.

To attain highest standard of procedures and practices followed by the corporate world so as to have transparency in it's functioning with an ultimate aim to maximize the value of various stakeholders.

It is possible through:

- building up an environment of trust and confidence amongst those having competing and conflicting interests and

- by enhancing shareholders' value and protecting the interest of other stakeholders by improving the corporate performance and accountability.

Corporate Governance is just another system of honesty in practice, until before the last decade of the yester century. However, the two cases in Indian context namely UTI's US64 and Enron operations have made an eye open to investors , stakeholders and for general public about the importance of corporate governance. In these cases the ultimate sufferers are small investors.

From the historical point of view so many reports like Coso (committee of sponsoring organization). Cadbury rutteman, Hampel, Turnbull etc., Naresh Chandra Committee, the Narayana Murthy Committee, Kumar Mangalam Birla Committee, etc; have revealed the importance of corporate governance for best business returns. However, majority of companies were victims of the "boom to bust" during the decade of 1980's. In this context there is every need to understand the practices of Corporate Governance in light LPG.

Since a decade plus, liberalization of the economy is developing highly competitive, volatile, complex and unpredictable business environment in India. Progressively, intense local and international competition is coming up. After the Liberalization, new markets, new alliances, new customers are emerging everyday. The Indian market is large and hence very attractive. As a consequence MNCs flooded the market. The companies from the developed countries, where they were facing a saturated market came to invest in India either as green field ventures (Samsung), acquiring an Indian business (Coca Cola, Heinz) or Joint Ventures (JVs) (Pal – Peugeot, Tata – IBM).

Initially JV was most popular, but that changed later (splits like Premier Automobiles—Automobile Peugeot, Tata and IBM, DCM and Daewoo). In the Indian condition, often the key was cheap labour, and hence the importance of having good senior management who were very aware of local conditions was great. Public Sector Units (PSUs) came under huge threat. Because, with liberalization, there came government divestment. The management came under pressure to show efficiency and profitability. And there was considerable brain drain—all the brighter PSU employees went to the private sector as job opportunities boomed. Family owned businesses were forced to turn professional or enter into contractual arrangements with larger houses.

Therefore, the key issue is how the Indian corporate sector can manage its business efficiently and effectively in this new era. Corporate Governance is a means of overcoming the absence of transparency and accountability as it seeks to minimize the malpractices by companies by establishing a system where more information about the transactions of the companies or decisions taken by the management are available to shareholders and public.

The switch towards Privatization in the last decade has increased the prominence of corporate governance because good corporate governance is indispensable for corporate success, prosperity, and competitiveness in an open and market driven economy. With the privatization, the PSU's will face different markets and business environment that would be more competitive, dynamic, and integrated with the world markets. That is why now-a-days many of the PSU's and private sectors are following the governance and able to turnaround their failures into successes.

In the era of Globalization and changing scenario of international business there is considerable debate about what actually constitutes corporate governance, however, there is consensus that its key factors include improved performance through monitoring and ensuring accountability of management to various stakeholders. This brings to focus the two distinct issues of ownership and accountability. Hence, corporate governance is about international, legal and cultural arrangement shaping the scope of the activities; the sources of control; and the manner in which the risks and returns are allocated.

Corporate Governance Initiatives in India

In India the issue of Corporate Governance has shot into prominence during the last decade or so because of the policy shift towards privatization and globalization because good corporate governance is indispensable for corporate success, prosperity and competitiveness in an open and market driven economy.

There have been several major Corporate Governance initiatives launched in India since the mid-1990s. The first was by the Confederation of Indian Industry (CII), India's largest industry and business association, which came up with the first voluntary code of corporate governance in 1998. The second was by the SEBI, now enshrined as Clause 49 of the listing agreement. The third was the

Naresh Chandra Committee, which submitted its report in 2002. The fourth was again by SEBI — the Narayana Murthy Committee, which also submitted its report in 2002. Based on some of the recommendation of this committee, SEBI revised Clause 49 of the listing agreement in August 2003.

Subsequently, SEBI withdrew the revised Clause 49 in December 2003, and currently, the original Clause 49 is in force.

CII set-up a committee to examine Corporate Governance issues, and recommended a voluntary code of best practices. The committee was driven by the conviction that good corporate governance was essential for Indian companies to access domestic as well as global capital at competitive rates. The first draft of the code was prepared by April 1997, and the final document (*Desirable Corporate Governance: A Code*), was publicly released in April 1998. The code was voluntary, contained detailed provisions, and focused on listed companies.

The chances of scams are always great during a period of globalization, when the economy is deregulated with a view to globalize at a rapid pace. One of the factors held responsible for the 1998 economic crisis in Asian countries was weak corporate governance.

Further, in a globalised business environment there is always a need for capital from the domestic as well as foreign sources. Under these circumstances any investor as well as creditor would like to ensure that his capital is safe and promises good return. This is the stage where governance in general and corporate governance in particularly, becomes very important and as such become the subject matter.

Shaping the Future Global System

Open economies, responsible corporate governance and corporate leadership are three essential components of a sustainable global system. Its objectives must be growth, adequate management of natural resources, access to and transfer of technology, participative policy-making process on a global scale, greater coherence between institutions and policies, dynamism, and regulation and policies adapted to real needs. Open economies, responsible corporate governance and corporate leadership are necessary and need to be closely correlated for these goals to be reached.

Conclusion

Corporate governance is a compulsion of long-term corporate existence. Its importance and significance get heightened due to globalization and liberalization. It is addressable factor for the success of globalization in an economy. Good corporate governance is necessity and for motivation towards progress. The Indian economy took a strategic shift at 1990's and now is in vigorous practice. Past experiences revealed the loopholes in the system because of which now Corporate Governance gained much prominence role. LPG is leading to grater transparency, accountability and responsibility.

The last decade witnessed the several scams considerably damaging the reputation of Indian corporate. No one would like to deal with trained companies, definitely the foreign investors and collaborators. If corporations in India want to survive and succeed in this competing global era, it can only be through corporate excellence, which in turn is impossible without sound corporate governance. In the present time of globalization the best results could be achieved when the companies begin to treat the code not as a mere structure, but as a way of life.

REFERENCES

Athreya, M.B. (2001), *Business Values for the 21st century*, in the Book "Corporate Governance and Business Ethics," All India Management Association, Excel Books, New Delhi, pp. 4-12.

Mohanty, Ashok, K. and Sahu, Promod, K. (Oct-Dec.,1998), *An Analysis of Corporate Governance in India*, Indian Journal of Commerce, p. 122.

Raju, R. Satya, *Corporate Governance in a Changing Environment*, Indian Mangement, March, 2000, Vol. 39.

Rangarajan, C. (1997), *Corporate Governance—The New Paradigm*, RBI Bulletin (October) 787.

Sarkar Jayati and Sarkar Subrata (1999), *The Governance of Indian Corporate in Kirit Parikh (ed.)*, Indian Development Report, 1999-2000, pp. 201-18.

21

Changing Financing Pattern of Indian Corporate Sector: Need for Strengthening Corporate Governance

Prof. P.V. Sarma & M.S.R. Seshagiri

Introduction

Conducting Business activities in the phase of Liberalization, Privatization and Globalization adhering to a set of social norms, popularly know as business ethics.

Nearly a year after the Enron revelations first surfaced, corporate governance dominates the political and business agenda. After a slew of scandals, most of them centered in the US, politicians and regulators, executives and shareholders are all preaching the governance gospel. Corporate governance is about how companies are directed and controlled. The balance sheet is an output of manifold structural and strategic decisions across the entire company, from stock options to risk management structures, from the composition of the board of directors to the decentralization of decision-making powers. As a result, the prime responsibility for good governance must be within the company rather than outside it.

The term "corporate governance" came out of a seminal analysis by two American academics in the 1920s who were looking at the growing separation of ownership and Control in the modern corporation. When ownership takes the form of disbursed shareholding, and professional managers take the place of the family structure or the government in running a company, there needs to be a system of control over those managers to ensure that the company is run in the interests of the shareholders.

Definition of Corporate Governance

"Corporate Governance is concerned with holding the balance between economic and social goals and between individual and communal goals. The corporate governance framework is there to encourage the efficient use of resources and equally to require accountability for the stewardship of those resources. The aim is to align as nearly as possible the interests of individuals, corporations and society."

"Corporate governance is a field in economics that investigates how to secure/motivate efficient management of corporations by the use of incentive mechanisms, such as contracts, organizational designs and legislation. This is often limited to the question of improving financial performance, for example, how the corporate owners can secure/motivate that the corporate managers will deliver a competitive rate of return."

"Corporate governance is a process or a set of systems and processes to ensure that a complaint is managed to suit the best interest of all, this may include structures and organizational matters."

Corporate Social Responsibility

Gandhi was a person who in several respects was ahead of his time. His view of the ownership of capital was one of trusteeship, motivated by the belief that essentially society was providing capitalists with an opportunity to manage resources that should really be seen as a form of trusteeship on behalf of society in general. Today, we are perhaps coming round full circle in emphasizing this concept through an articulation of the principle of social responsibility of business and industry.

While the interests of shareholders and the actions of managers of any business enterprise have to be governed by the laws of economics, requiring an adequate financial return on investments made, in reality the operations of an enterprise need to be driven by a much larger set of objectives that are today being defined under the term Corporate Social Responsibility (CSR). The broad rationale for a new set of ethics for corporate decision-making, which clearly constructs and upholds a company's social responsibility arises from the fact that a business enterprise derives several benefits from society, which must, therefore, require the enterprise to provide returns to society as well. Of course, the system of taxation in most countries does ensure that basic services provided by government such as a system of law and order, provision of infrastructure that includes assets such as roads, transportation facilities, the benefits received from the apparatus of society for respecting and enforcing property rights, etc., are paid for through taxation on economic goods and services produced and consumed. But there are other aspects of services provided by society that have now become even more important than traditional relationship between government and business. These go far beyond what was the case a few decades ago.

Why should companies whose major objective has been to maximize profits for the benefit of their shareholders worry at all about serving the interest of society at large? The answer is simple and yet somewhat circular in nature. A business cannot succeed in a society, which fails. This, therefore, clearly establishes the stake of a business organization in the good health and well-being of a society of which it is a part. More importantly, in this age of widespread communication and growing emphasis on transparency, customers of any product or service are unlikely to feel satisfied in buying from a company that is seen to violate the expectations of ethical and socially responsible behaviour. We find, therefore, that to a growing degree companies that pay genuine attention to the principles of socially responsible behaviour are also favoured by the public and preferred for their goods and services.

Need for Corporate Governance

Corporate governance is about the way in which boards oversee the running of a company by its managers, and how board members are in turn accountable to shareholders and the company. This has implications for company behaviour towards employees, shareholders, customers and banks. Good corporate governance plays a vital role in underpinning the integrity and efficiency of financial markets. Poor corporate governance weakens a company's potential and at worst can pave the way for financial difficulties and even fraud. If companies are well governed, they will usually outperform other companies and will be able to attract investors whose support can help to finance further growth.

"The proper governance of companies will become as crucial to the world economy as the proper governing of countries…. strong corporate governance produces good social progress. The two go together."

The financial capital flow across national borders creates necessity for the investors to ensure that the enterprises or the markets in which they are investing are not only managed competently that means they have good corporate management but also they are governed properly. The collapse of the South East Asian tiger economies like Thailand, South Korea, Malaysia, Indonesia in 1998 brought home the fact that if there is no proper corporate governance in the financial sector, it leads to corruption. This, in turn, leads to unsound investments, which are speculative and finally the investors lose.

Corporate governance depends upon two factors. The first is the commitment of the management for the principle of integrity and transparency in business operations. The second is the legal and the administrative framework created by the government. If public governance is weak, we cannot have good corporate governance. The dramatic Enron case has highlighted how companies, which were the hot stocks of the stock market and held up as models for vigorous and innovative growth can ultimately collapse like a house of cards as they were based on fraud and dishonesty. In the Indian context, the need for corporate governance has been highlighted because of the scams we have been having almost as an annual feature ever since we had liberalization.

Key Factors in Corporate Governance

1. Transparency in decision-making,
2. Accountability which follows from transparency because responsibilities could be fixed easily for actions taken or not taken, and
3. The accountability is for the safeguarding the interests of the stakeholders and the investors in the organization.

Analysis of Financing Pattern of Indian Corporate Sector–Foreign Holding Vs. Indian Holding

The sector-wise analysis of foreign holdings and the Indian holdings in the financial years 2001 to 2004 is presented in the Table 1.

The sector-wise analysis of the foreign and Indian holdings during the years 2001 to 2004 reveals that the foreign holding in the Indian companies is continuously increasing from 11.57 in the year

Table–1

Sectors	2001		2002		2003		2004	
	Foreign Holding	Indian Holding	Foreign Holding	Indian Holding	Foreign Holding	Indian Holding	Foreign Holding	Indian Holding
Finance	7.43	92.59	7.62	92.38	10.79	89.19	13.69	86.03
FMCG	54.97	45.03	57.81	42.02	57.23	42.76	52.14	47.87
Infrastructure	7.38	91.96	9.08	90.21	9.52	90.48	17.88	82.11
IT	16.51	83.49	14.79	85.23	18.75	81.24	14.71	85.29
Manufacturing	8.14	91.86	9.57	90.43	14.04	85.97	14.87	85.14
Media and Entertainment	3.99	96.00	26.09	73.09	17.03	82.98	11.22	88.79
Petrochemicals	7.01	93.00	4.93	95.07	5.18	94.82	6.09	93.91
Pharmaceuticals	18.27	81.73	14.46	85.54	9.41	90.58	16.74	83.27
Services	9.89	90.12	5.24	94.76	35.46	64.54	18.11	81.09
Telecommunication	35.08	64.91	28.04	71.61	20.31	79.69	10.07	89.91
Miscellaneous	5.55	94.45	9.47	90.52	14.43	85.76	12.34	87.66
All Companies	11.57	88.41	13.03	86.96	15.89	84.11	14.95	85.05

2001 to 14.95 in the year 2004 per cent. In the case of FMCG section a consistent increase of Foreign holding may be observed between there consecutive years. However, an examination of infrastructure also reveals the same that from a Foreign holding of 7.38 per cent has increased to 17.88 per cent in consecutive years (2001-04). Even at manufacturing sector Foreign holding has increased from 8.14 per cent to 14.87 per cent. An abnormal change is observed during the year 2002 in media and entertainment sector i.e., a steep raise of 22.10 per cent from just 3.99 per cent in 2001. But the same is not continued and dropped to 11.22 per cent by the year 2004. In the row Petrochemical Sector is the one where Foreign holding is consistently increased from 4.93 per cent in 2002 to 6.09 per cent in 2004. In the service sector Foreign holding touched 35.46 per cent in 2003 compared to 5.24 per cent in 2002 year. Telecommunications sector is very distinct compared to all the above motioned sectors where Foreign holding has consistently reduced from 35.08 per cent (2001) to 10.07 per cent (2004) i.e., a variation of 25.01 per cent. The analysis signifies that the raising foreign holding in the Indian companies highlights the need for greater transperancy and strengthing of the corporate governance practices of the companies.

Analysis of Financing Pattern of Indian Corporate Sector–Promoters Holding Vs. Non-Promoters Holding

The sector-wise analysis of foreign holdings and the Indian holdings in the financial years 2001 to 2004 is presented in the Table 2.

Table–2

Sectors	2001		2002		2003		2004	
	Non-Promoters Holding	Promoters Holding	Non-Promoters Holding	Promoters Holding	Non-Promoters Holding	Promoters Holding	Non-Promoters Holding	Promoters Holding
Finance	54.59	45.43	50.68	49.32	50.00	49.98	50.91	49.08
FMCG	51.05	48.05	47.07	52.94	47.06	52.39	45.54	54.47
Infrastructure	66.38	32.96	57.18	42.83	44.63	55.37	49.69	50.03
IT	57.63	42.37	59.26	40.74	66.94	33.05	56.68	43.32
Manufacturing	36.87	63.13	38.21	61.79	43.51	56.05	40.12	59.89
Media and Entertainment	93.63	6.36	51.32	48.67	41.98	58.03	43.69	56.32
Petrochemicals	39.74	60.27	38.45	61.55	39.79	60.21	35.12	64.88
Pharmaceuticals	50.23	49.77	53.65	46.35	43.02	56.79	49.99	50.02
Services	44.58	55.43	43.35	56.65	50.12	49.88	47.63	52.38
Telecommunication	47.13	52.86	44.35	55.66	52.54	47.46	45.13	54.85
Miscellancous	38.01	61.99	54.56	45.43	53.19	47.00	51.57	48.43
All Companies	49.04	50.94	44.47	55.52	46.81	53.19	44.37	55.63

The sector-wise analysis of the promoters and non-promoters holdings during the years 2001 to 2004 reveals that the non-promoters holding in the Indian companies is varying between 49.04 per cent to 46.81 per cent during the years 2001 to 2004. In FMCG sector Non-promoters Holding is reduced to 45.54 per cent in 2004 from 51.5 per cent in 2001, a variation of 6.1 per cent. In Infrastructure too Non-Promoters Holding is reduced around 16 per cent from 66.38 per cent in 2001 to 50.30 per cent at 2004. In the IT sector, the non-promoters holding increased from 57.63 per cent in the year 2001 to 66.94 per cent in the year 2003 but in the year 2004 it has reduced to 56.68 per cent. However, in the manufacturing sector Non-promoters Holding has raised from 36.87 per cent in 2001 to 43.51 per cent in 2003. A completely different scenario is observed at Media and Entertainment Sector during the year 2001, where more than 90 per cent in Non-promoters Holding which gradually reduced to 43.69 per cent by the year 2004. At Petrochemical sector there is no considerable variations on either side. The analysis of the promoters and non-promoters holding in the Indian corporate sectors too signifies the need for greater transparency and more accountability in safeguarding the interests of the stakeholders of the company.

Conclusion

With the increasing participation of the foreign investors and raising contribution of the non-promoters in financing Indian companies, the Indian corporate sector should take necessary measures in protecting the interests of the stakeholders. The government should also strengthen the corporate governance-related reporting by the Indian companies to ensure the compliance of the Indian companies in maintaining global standards in corporate governance practices.

REFERENCES

1. *Corporate Governance, What it means and what is needs,* Management Review, July-Dec., 1996.
2. *C.G. World Wide,* Management Review, July-Dec., 1996.
3. *Corporate Governance: What Needs to be Done,* Fortune India, January 16-31, 1997.
4. *Corporate Governance: Multi-faceted Issue,* Chartered Secretary, May, 1997.
5. *Proceedings of Silver Jubilee National Convention of ICSI,* Chartered Secretary, October 1997.
6. *Corporate Governance, Time for a Metamorphosis,* The Hindu, July 9, 1997.
7. *Business Today,* May 7-21, 1997.
8. N. Gopalaswamy, *Corporate Governance – The New Paradigm,* Wheeler Publishing, A Division of A.H. Wheeler and Co., Ltd., New Delhi, 1998.
9. Indian Banks Association, Indian Banking Book, Mumbai 2003.
10. Vepakesam, "Corporate Governance", Reserve Bank of India Bulletin, January 2000, pp. 21-43.

22

Corporate Governance and Indian Experience

Prof. B. Appa Rao, K. Nageswara Rao and G. Srinivasa Rao

PART–I

Introduction

The term "Corporate Governance", although now common place, was rarely encounter before the 1990s. In its narrowest sense the term may describe the formal system of accountability of senior management to the shareholders.

If its most expansive the term is stretched to include the entire network of formal and informal relations involving the corporate sector and their consequences for society in general. Corporate Governance includes 'the structures, process, cultures, and systems that engender the successful operation of the organizations.' In the corporate governance debate, there is an increasing emphasis on the need for institutional shareholders to play an active role in the governance of companies. Corporate Governance has attracted worldwide attention in recent times and is gaining furtherer momentum because of the changing business environment all over the world. There has been a growing international focus on Corporate Governance particularly in the wake of worldwide financial turbulence, which manifested in the economic crises in some parts of East Asia, Russia, Japan and Latin America. The experience in these countries as also in our country over the years seemed to have proved the inadequacy of law to bring the best out of corporate management and a need was felt for a comprehensive code of Corporative Governance. The establishment of EEC, GATT and WTO regulations has also led to increased awareness about the need to adhere to good corporate practices. As a consequence, the corporate scene all over the world has witnessed phenomenal changes marked by re-structuring, mergers and acquisitions, takeover, strategic alliances etc. Significantly, the issue of public accountability through Corporate Governance has been brought into sharp focus by these changes.

PART–II

Evolution of the Concept

The emergence of large corporations during the middle and later part of the 20th century brought in distinctive categories of stakeholders in the company in contrast with the earlier system of owners managing the company. While shareholders contributed the capital, the managers were charged with the responsibility of running the show to achieve the set goals of the corporation. Customers also started receiving due importance as their loyalty to and patronage of the company was crucial for its prosperity. In doing this, human resources were essential and the employees too gained prominence as stakeholders. With the realization of the concept of corporate citizen, responsibility to the society also became a relevant issue. When different categories of stakeholders came to be identified, it became necessary to take care of each one's interests. It was also necessary to harmonize the divergent interests so that the corporation could endure pressures of anyone group. A code of practices that could be adopted in running the affairs of the company came to be evolved. These practices did not have necessarily a legal sanction but the compulsions of managing a large corporation facilitated the evolution of what came to be recognized as best practices.

The Concept

It is difficult to describe precisely the concept of Corporate Governance. But in essence it stands for "effective accountability to all stakeholders. In a normative sense, corporate governance prescribes a code of corporate conduct in relation to all the stakeholders, external as well as internal. It also provides the structure through which a company sets its corporate goals, decides the paths towards achieving them and monitors the performance on an ongoing basis. It goes to the credit of the Cadbury Committee to give the concept a form and a substance and more importantly a definition.

According to the Cadbury Committee, set-up in May, 1991, "Corporate Governance is a system by which companies are directed and controlled." Malegam elucidates this definition further by starting that there are two important clauses in this definition. First, it is a system and so everyone who is a part of the system is contributing towards Corporate Governance. Secondly, it is a system by which companies are directed and controlled, not managed on a day-to-day basis.

According to the Organization for Economic Cooperation and Development (OECD) corporate governance involves set of relationships between a company's management, its board, its shareholders and other stakeholders. These principles codified in June 1999 were earlier highlighted by the Cadbury' Committee set-up by the London Stock Exchange (LSE) in1992. The companies registered in LSE were required to report the extent of their compliance with the Cadbury code in their annual reports. The thrust of Cadbury Committee was on openness, integrity and accountability.

According to L.V.V. Ayer "Corporate Governance can be defined as a set of systems and processes which ensure that a company is managed to the best interest of all the stakeholders. The set systems that help the task of corporate governance should include certain structural and organizational aspects; the process that helps corporate governance will embrace how things are done within such structure and organizational system."

In his 'Role of Board of Directors in Emerging Dimensions', Dr. K. R. Chandratre has explained the concept in the following words: "(Corporate Governance) is the expression which is not capable of being precisely defined. However, broadly speaking, corporate governance denotes direction and control of the affairs of a company." "The role of corporate governance is to ensure that the directors of a company are subject to their duties, obligations and responsibilities, to act in the best interest of their company, to give direction and remain accountable to their shareholders and other beneficiaries for their actions." (Corporate Governance and Corporate Control, Salim Sheikh and William Ress, 1995). Corporate Governance is also concerned with the ethics, values and moral of a company and its directors.

Similar views also have been offered by Dr. Narang in his Development of Corporate Governance in India: "Corporate Governance is a broad and somewhat vague term used to refer to a range of corporate controls and accountability mechanisms designed to meet the aims of corporate stockholders. Corporate governance has also been defined to cover the concepts, theories and practices of board and its directors, and the relationships between board and the shareholders. Thus, corporate governance, as is generally understood, is the process of direction, supervision and accountability of corporations."

Ingredients of Corporate Governance

The definition given by OECD contains the essential ingredients of corporate governance. The following issues are relevant:

1. It provides the structure through which the objectives of the company are set.
2. It prescribes the means of attaining those objectives.
3. It determines the method of monitoring the performance.

To further quote the OECD paper 1 "Good Corporate Governance should provide proper incentives to the board and management to pursue objectives that are in the interests of the company and shareholders, and should facilitate effective monitoring, thereby encouraging firms to use recourses more efficiently."

If the objectives of the company are to be achieved, there should be appropriate checks and controls, division of responsibility and disclosure and transparency. These measures, however, were already in place in different forms before the concept gained the current level of importance. For instance, the audit was intended to ensure that the company followed certain sound financial and accounting practices, the board of directors was charged with the responsibility of ensuring the compliance of all statutory requirements. There were statutory bodies to monitor compliance. Yet it became necessary to codify the practices to provide a self-contained mechanism for the efficient working of the company.

PART–III

Need for Corporate Governance

In the wake of globalization, liberalization, Privatization and financial sector reforms as also the establishment of World Trade Organization (WTO) to which our country is also signatory, the economy of our country has been becoming more and more open economy making the entry of worldwide countries easier. The implication of WTO agreement for developing countries like of ours, is removal of tariff and non-tariff barriers to improve market access for partner countries signifying that protectionism has become a thing of the past. No doubt, various concessions relating to time-frame and tariff, non-tariff barriers have been given to the developing countries like of ours, it is a fact that the country will be able to gain from the global free-trade marked by reduced barriers only when the Indian corporates learn to govern and manage their financial and non-financial affairs most efficiently. With these liberalization/globalization measures, facilitating increased flow of foreign direct investment in different sectors of the economy, Indian corporates would not be able to avoid the rigours of International regulation and many of the best business practices prevalent in developed countries.

Good Corporate Governance enhances the image/reputation of the corporate and helps it as a user of the capital, to build long-term relationship with those who are stakeholders in the business of the corporate. With the trans-nationalization of the financial markets, Corporate Governance is used as a marketing tool to top International capital markets to raise required capital at lowest possible rates.

Corporate Governance in India

On like other Asian countries, the initial thrust for more disclosure and better Corporate Governance came in India mainly due to the 1992 Stock market scan and the onset of International competition resulting from the policy of liberalization of the economy in 1991. There has been a growing concern about good Corporate Governance in the corporate sector to gain investor confidence specially in the after math of corporate failures and financial irregularities which exposed the lack of adequate management accountability. Although the Governance framework necessarily depends on the prevailing corporate structures, Legal Framework and Socio-culture climate of a country, nevertheless the core principles by and large remain the same everywhere rightly so in these days of Globalization. Keeping this in view, the Confederation of Indian Industries (CII) took the lead and was the first to appoint a committee under the chairmanship of Mr. Rahul Bajaj in 1998 as a national level private initiative to evolve desirable rules for corporate Governance. The CII took the lead in framing a voluntary code of desirable corporate Governance practices in April, 1998 containing recommendations regarding the composition of the Board of Directors, levels of corporate disclosures, Role of Audit Committee and other related matters and enhancing corporate transparency and responsibility. Subsequently, the subject was hotly debated amongst industry and trade associations, government and academia. This was followed by appointment of as many as four more National Level Committees—Two appointed by SEBI, namely Kumar Mangalam Birla Committee in 1999 and N. R. Narayana Murthy Committee in 2003, another Committee on financial sector governance, popularly known as Ganguly Committee report in 2002 and the fourth Committee appointed by the Government of India known as Report of the Naresh Chandra Committee on Corporate Audit and Governance, in December 2002. This shows beyond doubt that both industry associations and the Government of India, on the other hand, and the banking regulator (the Reserve Bank of India) and company regulator (SEBI) on the other, are equally interested in putting Corporate Governance practices in India on an even pedestal with anywhere else in the world.

Theories of Corporate Governance

Based on the Ownership pattern of the Company, Corporate Governance theories can be classified into three types. These are:

1. Indo-Asian Model.
2. Anglo-American Model.
3. German-Japanese Model.

Indo-Asian Model (PDSHM)

Under this model, an enlightened dominant promoter would generally have long range enlightened vision for decades, for the company. Generally, the promoter shareholders would empathize for retail shareholders also and align his interest with their own. This will ensure a smooth growth for the company for a vary long period. It is possible, that the promoters, their kin and kith, friends and relatives, etc., may derive both financial and non-financial benefits from the company, but may keep their shareholders' happy by creating a sustained Economic Value Addition (EVA) over a long period. This model runs very effectively and successfully during the life of founder-promoter or may be during the period of next generation but next may rarely be lucky to sustain the growth or even arrest the decline. Tatas of India seem to be an exception in this regard.

However, while constituting the board of these companies, care has to be taken that majority of the directors are independent, knowledgeable and dependable persons so as to ensure that economic justice acerues to the retail shareholders and stakeholders of the company.

Anglo-American Model

Under this model, serving the shareholders is the dominate goal of companies in these two countries. The layer of management and governance is integrated into one super body, i.e., Board. The directorial principles of forming a will, i.e.: The Chief Executive Officer (CEO) has strong executive powers relative to the other top management of the company.

In this model the corporation may excel in overall performance. But one has to take care that no close nexus develops between the CEO and the Chief Financial Officer (CFO). Lest the two create an Enron-type situation of boom and bust in no time.

German-Japanese Model

The German corporate governance model was characterized by the importance of banks, ownership concentration, long-term investment and relatively stable corporate networks. This system displayed important complementaries with long -term employment, investment in skill up gradation of workers, flexible quality production, low variability and dispersion in pay and very harmonious and cooperative industrial relations during the post-war periods. Since the mid-1990's, corporate governance has changed dramatically—a decline in the role of banks, the unwinding of the corporate networks, the rise of Foreign Institutional Investors (FIIs), emerging market for corporate control and changing careers and compensation of top managers. This has also emphasized greater need for shareholder-value management practices, which may ultimately benefit the employees, as well as the economy as a whole.

PART–IV

Cadbury Committee

In early 1990s in UK, there was mounting criticism of the quality of financial reporting and the effectiveness of the independent auditing. This led to the establishment of a committee on financial aspects of corporate governance (known as Cadbury Committee), which reported in late 1992 and again in 1996.

The first report of Cadbury Committee, which had the backing of the Bank of England, the London Stock Exchange and the Accounting Bodies, sought to establish a Code of Best Practice on disclosure and audit arrangements. Companies listed on the Stock Exchange were required to make a statement in their annual report that they compiled with the Code Best Practice. So this aspect of corporate governance was exercised not through statute but in 'voluntary' way—albeit with server penalties for non-compliance.

It is interesting to note that the single issue which attracted most attention was the disclosure of directors' pay. This was the subject of a separate report in the UK—the Greenbury Report. This indicated the need for corporate governance arrangements to address issues where there is potentially a conflict of interest.

The Cadbury Committee identified three fundamental principles of good corporate governance, namely openness, integrity and accountability. From the suggestions given by the Cadbury Committee two things are evident:

1. First, they key to good corporate governance is a well-functioning board of directors. The board should have a core group of excellent, professionally acclaimed non-executive directors who understand their dual role of appreciating the issues put forward by management and of honestly discharging their fiduciary responsibilities towards the company's shareholders as well as creditors.
2. Second, corporate governance goes beyond the economy law and covers the quantity, quality and frequency of financial and managerial disclosure, the extent to which the board of directors exercise their fiduciary responsibilities towards shareholders and the quality of information that the management share with their board.

The Cadbury code stresses that where the chairman of the board also happens to be the chief executive, "it is essential that there should be a strong independent element on the Board, with recognized senior members."

As stated above, the issues of Corporate Governance that emanated primarily for the Cadbury—Committee Report (Cadbury, 1996), UK found favour in other countries as well Cadbury Committee clearly mentioned that Corporate Governance has three important pillars. These are: Nomination Committee; Remuneration Committee and The Audit Committee.

Blue Ribbon Committee

The Blue Ribbon Committee recommends that in addition to adopting the definition of independence set fourth, the NYSE and the National Association of Securities Dealers (NASD) require that the listed companies with a market capitalization above $200 million. Have an audit committee comprised solely of independent directors.

The Blue Ribbon Committee also suggested the following other measures for improving efficacy of the audit:

I. Adoption of a written charter of activities approved by a full board specifying responsibilities of the audit committee.

II. Annual public disclosure of activities carried out by the audit committee. Audit committee as the representative of the shareholders should have the authority to propose appointment and replacement of the outside auditors.

III. Audit committee should enjoy the full authority of carrying out discussion with the auditors and the board should ensure complete independence of the outside auditors. This should form part o' the listing agreement.

IV. The Generally Accepted Auditing Standards (GAAS) in the USA require that a company's outside auditor discuss with the audit committee the auditor's judgements about the quality, not just the acceptability, of the company's accounting principles clarity of the company's financial disclosures and degree of aggressiveness or conservatism of the company's accounting principles and underlying estimates and other significant decisions made by management in preparing the financial disclosures and reviewed by the outside auditors. This should form part of the required ambience to encourage frank discussion.

V. The Committee recommends that the SEC require all reporting companies to include a letter from the audit committee in the company's annual report to shareholders and Form 1 G-K Annual Report disclosing whether or not, with respect to the prior fiscal year; *(i)* management has reviewed the audited financial statements with the audit committee, including a discussion of the quality of the accounting principles as applied and significant judgements affecting the company's financial statements; *(ii)* the outside auditors have discussed with the audit committee the outside auditor's judgements of the quality of those principles; *(iii)* the members of the audit committee have discussed among themselves, without management or the outside auditors present, the information disclosed to the audit committee, and *(iv)* the audit committee believes that the company's financial statement are fairly presented in conformity with Generally Accepted Accounting Principle (GAAP) in all material respects.

VI. The Committee recommends that the SEC require that a reporting company's outside auditor conduct an SAS 71 Interim Financial Review prior to the company's filing of its Form 10-Q return.

OECD'S PRINCIPLES OF GOOD CORPORATE GOVERNANCE

OECD has developed the following five principles of good corporate governance:

Protect Shareholders Rights

I. Shareholders should have the opportunity to participate effectively, vote in general shareholder meetings and should be informed of the rules, including voting procedures that govern shareholder meetings.

II. Capital structures and arrangements that enable certain shareholders to obtain a degree of control disproportionate to their equity ownership should be disclosed.

III. Markets for corporate control should be a allowed to function in an efficient and transparent manner.

Equitable Treatment of Shareholders

The corporate governance framework should ensure the equitable treatment of all shareholders, including minority and foreign shareholders. All shareholders should have the opportunity to obtain effective redress for violation of their rights. Insider trading and abusive self-dealing should be prohibited.

Role of Stakeholders in Corporate Governance

The corporate governance framework should recognize the rights of stakeholders as established by law and encourage active co-operation between corporations and stakeholders in creating wealth jobs end. The sustainability of financially should enterprises.

Responsibility of the Board

The corporate framework should ensure the strategic guidance of the company, the effective monitoring of management by the board and the board's accountability to the company and the shareholders.

Board members should act on a fully informed basis, in good faith, with due diligence and care, and in the best interest of the company and the shareholders. Where board decisions may affect different shareholder groups differently, the board should treat all shareholders fairly. The board should also ensure compliance with applicable law and take account the interests of stakeholders.

Further, the board should fulfill certain key functions including:

I. Reviewing and guiding corporate strategy, major plans of action, risk policy, annual budgets and business plans; setting performance objectives; monitoring, implementation and corporate performance; and overseeing major capital expenditures, acquisition and divestitures.

II. Selecting, compensating, monitoring and when necessary, replacing key executives and overseeing succession planning.

III. Reviewing key executive and board remuneration, and ensuring a formal and transparent board nomination process.

IV. Monitoring and managing potential conflicts of interest of management, board members and shareholders, including misuse of corporate assets and abuse in related party transactions.

V. Ensuring the integrity of the corporation's accounting and financial reporting systems, including the independent audit, and that appropriate systems of control are in place, in particular, systems for monitoring risk, financial control, and compliance with the law.

VI. Monitoring the effectiveness of the governance practices under which it operates and making changes as needed.

VII. Overseeing the process of disclosure and communications.

The board should be able to exercise objective judgement on corporate affairs independent, in particular, from management Boards should consider assigning a sufficient number of non-executive board members capable of exercising independent judgment to tasks where there is a potential for conflict of interest. Examples *of such* key responsibilities are financial reporting, nomination and executive and board remuneration. Members should devote sufficient time to their responsibilities.

In order to fulfill their responsibilities, board members should have access to accurate, relevant and timely information.

Disclosure and Transparency

Corporate framework should ensure that timely and accurate disclosure is made on all material matters, including the financial situation, performance, ownership and governance of the company. Information should be prepared, audited and disclosed in accordance with high quality standards of accounting, financial and non-financial disclosure and audit. An annual audit should also be conducted by an independent auditor in order to provide an external and objective assurance on way in which financial statements have been prepared and presented.

Desirable Corporation Governance in India—A Code (CII Task Force Committee), 1998

The Confederation of Indian Industries (CII) was the first to appoint a committee under the chairmanship of Mr. Rahul Bajaj in 1998 as a National level private initiative to evolve desirable rules for corporate governance.

CII Task Force Report: Desirable Disclosure

The text of the Draft Report on Corporate Governance released by the Confederation of Indian Industry also has elaborately dealt with the desirable disclosure by companies. Apart from listing selected key information which must be reported to, and placed before the

Board, the report also has listed various times of non-financial disclosures and financial disclosures, as listed and recommended by the Working Group on the Companies Act. The Task Force Report has recommended that though the disclosures recommended by the Working Group in its report as well as in the modified Schedule VI that would accompany the Draft Bill can go far beyond existing levels, more needs to be done outside the framework of law, particularly; *(i)* A model of voluntary disclosure in the current context, and *(ii)* Consolidation of accounts. The report recommends 'Addition Shareholders' 'Information', in the case of listed companies and data covering the following:

(i) High and low monthly averages of share process at all the Stock Exchanges where the company is listed for the reporting year.

(ii) Statement on value added which is total income minus the cost of all inputs and administrative expenses.

(iii) Greater details on business segments or division, upto 5 per cent of turnover, giving share in sales revenue, share in contribution, review of operations analysis of markets and future prospects.

The Working Group on the Companies Act has recommended that consolidation should be optional and not mandatory. The Task Force also recommends consolidation of group accounts being made optional and subject to the FIs allowing companies to leverage on the basis of the group's assets and the Income-Tax Department using the group concept in assessing corporate Income-Tax. The Task Force has also recommended that major Indian Stock Exchanges should gradually insist upon a compliance certificate, signed by the CEO and CFO, stating that the management is responsible for the preparation, integrity and fair presentation of the financial statements and other information in the Annual Report, and that the accounting policies and principles conform to standard practice and the board has overseen the company's system of internal accounting and administrative controls.

The Task Force, referring to tapping of the GDR markets, has commented that it will not be credible to present, one set of accounts to investors in New York and Washington DC, and a completely different one to the shareholders in the country. There is something inequitable about a company disclosing substantially more for its GDR issue compared to its domestic issue. It has accordingly recommended that in the case of all companies with paid-up capital of Rs. 20 crore, or more, the quality and quantity of disclosure that accompanies a GDR issue should be the norm for any domestic issue. The Task Force has further stated: "With the country moving into an era of a fully convertible capital account and Indian companies aspiring to be major players in the global financial markets, it is essential for domestic companies to move on to Generally Accepted Accounting Principles (GAAP) and to adopt transparent accounting norms." The report has preferred Indian companies routinely giving in a detailed and readable manner—the accounting principles that govern fixed assets, depreciation, revenue, revenue expenditure on R & D, inventories, investments that are expected to be liquidated in a year, earnings from investments, transactions in foreign currency, proposed dividend, retirement benefits, contingencies and non-recurring revenue expenditure.

All listed companies should give their shareholders a graph plotting share price movement throughout the year and a table that gives the dates and values of the peaks and troughs. This should be plotted against the SSE Sensex and the NSE-50 index, which are the main market indicators. The report has also called for separate disclosure with details regarding debt performance, interest costs and the state of receivables as well as a separate disclosure for foreign exchange risks and exposure. Similarly, there should be separate reports on any major outstanding litigation the company is engaged in, as well as a report on the remuneration of the Chairman and all directors and senior managers.

The SEBI Committee on Corporate Governance, 2000

The Securities and Exchange Board of India (SEBI) had appointed a committee on Corporate Governance, on May 7, 1999 under the chairmanship of Shri Kumar Mangalam Birla, member SEBI Board, to Promote and raise the standards of Corporate Governance. The committee had submitted its report in February, 2000.

The Committee has reviewed the fundamental objective of corporate governance as enhancement of shareholders' value. Keeping in the view the interests of the other stakeholders. It has identified three key constituents of the corporate governance:

1. Shareholders.
2. Board of Directors.
3. Management.

In the concept of corporate governance role of these three important groups are defined along with their rights and responsibilities. The committee has made wide range of recommendations on various aspects of company management viz.

Composition of board of directors

Appointment of nominee directors by banks and financial institutions Role of independent directors

Setting up of an audit committee

Setting up of remuneration committee.

Stipulation of accounting standards and financial reporting level of disclosures relating to important financial and commercial transactions and shareholders rights.

The report of the committee is the first formal and comprehensive attempt to evolve a Code of Corporate Governance, in the context of prevailing conditions of governance in Indian companies, as well as the state of capital markets. While making the recommendations the Committee has been mindful that any code of Corporate Governance must be dynamic, evolving and should change with changing context and times. This code is to be reviewed from time-to-time, with the changing expectation of the investors, shareholders, and other stakeholders and with increasing sophistication achieved in capital markets.

The code of corporate governance should be followed by all listed companies, their directors, management, employees and professionals associated with such companies. This code should be followed by them both in letter and spirit and should always be in a manner that gives precedence to substance over form. The ultimate responsibility for putting the Code into practices lies directly with the board of directors of the company. The listed entities, which are not companies, but body corporates (e.g., private and public sector banks, financial institutions, insurance companies etc) incorporated under other statutes, the code of corporate governance shall apply to the extent that they do not violate their respective statutes, and guidelines or directives issued by the relevant regulatory authorities.

Report of the Consultative Group of Director of Banks and Financial Institution, 2002

The Consultative Group of Directors of Banks and Financial Institutions was set-up by the Reserve Bank in consultation with ISA, under the chairmanship of Dr. A.S. Ganguly, Director, Central Board, Reserve Bank of India in 2001.

The Group reviewed the existing legal framework governing constitution of the board of banks and financial institutions such as appointment of the Chairmen and Managing Directors of banks, appointment of independent directors and of auditors, etc. The Group looked into the functioning of the boards of banks, the quality of information flow to the boards, the system prevailing in banks for the follow up of the action taken on the earlier decisions of the board, compliance with legal and regulatory requirements. Secretarial practices relating to Board matters, etc. The Group also reviewed contemporary literature on the subject and the international best practices such as those enunciated by the Basel Committee on Banking supervision, the OECD. The guidelines issued by the Hong Kong Monetary Authority, the recommendations of the Kumar Mangalam Birla Committee appointed by the SEBI, recommendations of the Advisory Groups set-up by RBI on Corporate Governance (under the chairmanship of Dr. R.H. Patil) and on Banking Supervision (under the chairmanship of Shri M.S.Verma). A note indicating the principles I recommendations (as applicable to banks) arising out of the best practices as also of the reports of the aforesaid Groups was circulated among the banks for their comments. The comments received from banks and financial institutions were considered by the Group and taken into account to the extent relevant to the terms of reference while formulating its recommendations.

Ganguly Committee has suggested the formation of the following committees of the Board, in addition to the nomination committee: Audit Committee, Shareholders' Redressal Committee, Supervisory Committee and Risk Management Committee. The job of the first two committees is well-known in all bit corporates in India. Incidentally, RBI has prescribed that the Audit Committee should be presided over by a Chartered Accountant Director. But Ganguly

Committee opines that it could be done by any non-executive director. This is a move in the right direction.

Ganguly Committee has rightly observed that the present remuneration in the form of sitting fees is quite low for the work expected of Directors. One way of rewarding them is to give them a share in the profits and another is to give them share options in the bank. The Committee has suggested share options. This needs urgent consideration by the RBI. Of course, there is one danger that, like some of the top managers in failed companies in USA, the Board might pursue short-term profits, at the expense of long-term stability; in some cases, there could be a temptation to boost profits by manipulating accounts. One possible way of curbing it, is to stipulate a lock in period of 3 or 4 years for such share options. A question may arise as to whether even the nominees of RBI and Government should be entitled to such remuneration. The answer is that RBI should not have their nominees at all, as suggested by the second Narasimham Committee on banking sector reforms, because a regulator cannot done the role of participant also. Government should preferably withdraw their nominees from boards of public sector banks and monitor performance only through periodical reports. It is a recorded fact that many such banks faced massive losses, even when Government and RBI nominees were on the Boards.

Committee on Corporate Audit and Governance, 2002

Given below are the important recommendations of the Committee:

Disqualification of Audit Assignments

(a) Prohibition of any direct financial interest in the audit client by the audit firm, its partners or members of the engagement team as well as their direct relatives.

(b) Prohibition of receiving any loans and/or guarantees from or on behalf of the audit client by the audit firm, its partners or any member of the engagement team and their 'direct relatives.'

(c) Prohibition of any business relationship with the audit client by the auditing firm, its partners or any member of the engagement team and their 'direct relatives'.

List of Prohibited Non-Audit Services

(a) Prohibition of undue dependence. Where an audit firm has subsidiary, associate of affiliated entities, yardstick of no more that 25 per cent of revenues coming from a single audit client stated in recommendation 2.1 should be widened to accommodate the consolidated entity.

(b) The other prohibitions listed in recommendation 2.1 should also apply in full to all affiliated consulting and specialized service entities of any audit firm that are either subsidiaries of the audit firm, or have common ownership of over 50 per cent with the audit firm. And all the tests of independence outlined in recommendation 2.1 should be carried over to the consolidated entity.

Compulsory Audit Partner Rotation

(a) There is no need to legislate in favour of compulsory notation of audit firms.

(b) Also, in line with the provisions of the European Union and the IFAC, persons who are compulsorily rotated could, if need be, allowed to return after a break of three years.

Auditing the Auditors

Setting-up of Independent Quality Review Board

There should be established, with appropriate legislative support, three independent Quality Review Boards (QRB), one each for the ICAI, the ICSI and ICWAI, to periodically examine the review the quality of audit, secretarial and cost accounting firms and pass judgement and comments on the quality and sufficiency of systems, infrastructure and practices.

Proposed Disciplinary Mechanism for Auditor

Classification of offences and merging of schedules: At present there are two schedules of offences and misconduct—with the second schedule requiring action by High Courts.

Independent Directors

Defining an Independent Director

An employee, executive director or nominee of any bank, financial institution, corporations or trustees of debenture and bond holders, who is normally called a 'nominee director' will be excluded from the pool of director in the determination of the number of independent director. In other words, such as director will not figure either in the numerator or the denominator.

Percentage of Independent Director

No less that 50 per cent of the board of directors of any listed company, as well as unlisted public limited companies with a paid-u share capital and free reserve of Rs. 10 crore and above, or turnover of Rs. 50 crore and above, should consist of independent director independence being defined.

Tele-conferencing and Video Conferencing

The Committee noted that both the 1997 Report on the Working Group on the Companies Act, and Clause 49 of listing agreement list out, adequately, the information that must be placed before the board of directors. To ensure that asymmetry of information for stakeholders, especially shareholders, is not further enhanced/ reduced, the committee recommends.

Audit Committee Charter

In addition to disclosing the names of members of the Audit Committee and the dates and frequency of meetings, the Chairman of the Audit Committee must annually certify whether and to what extent each of the functional listed in the Audit Committee Charter were discharged I the course of the year. This will serve as the 'Committee's action taken' report to the shareholders.

Remuneration of Non-Executive Director

The statutory limit on sitting fees should be reviewed, although ideally it should be a matter to be resolved between the management and the shareholders.

Exempting Non-Executive Directors form Certain Liabilities

The time has come to insert provisions in the definition chapters of certain Acts specifically exempt non-executive and independent directors from such criminal and civil liabilities.

Training of Independent Directors

DCA should encourage institutions of prominence including their proposed Center for Corporate Excellence to have regular training programmes for independent director. In framing the programmes, and for other preparatory work, funding could possibly come from the IEPF.

The Report of the SEBI Committee on Corporate Governance, 2002

SEBI constituted a committee on corporate governance in December, 2002 under the chairmanship of Shri N.R. Narayana Murthy, Chairman and Chief Mentor of Infosys Technologies Limited. The Committee deliberated various issues related to Corporated Governance and submitted its Report on 8 February, 2003.

Mandatory Recommendation

1. All audit committee members should be "financially literate- and at least one member should have accounting or related financial management expertise."
2. In case of company has followed a treatment different from that prescribed in an accounting standard, management should justify why they believe such alternative treatment is more representative of the underlying business transaction. Management should also clearly explain the alternative accounting treatment in the footnotes to the financial statements.
3. Companies should be encouraged to move towards a regime of unqualified financial statements. This recommendation should be reviewed at an appropriate juncture to determine whether the financial reporting climate is conducive towards system of filing only unqualified financial statements.
4. A statement of all transactions with related parties including their bases should be placed before the independent audit committee for formal approval/ratification. If any transaction is not on an arm's length basis, management should provide an explanation to the audit committee justifying the same.
5. The term "related party" shall have the same meaning as contained in Accounting Standard 18, Related Party Transactions, issued by the Institute of Chartered Accountants of India.
6. Procedures should be in place to inform Board members about the risk assessment and minimization procedures.

These procedures should be periodically reviewed to ensure that executive management controls risk through means of a properly defined framework. Management should place a report before the entire Board of Directors every quarter documenting the business risks faced by the company, measures to address and minimize such risks, and any limitations to the risk taking capacity of the corporation. This document should be formally approved by the Board.

7. Companies should be encouraged to train their Board members in the business model of the company as well as the risk profile of the business parameters of the company, their responsibilities as directors, and the best ways to discharge them.

8. Companies raising money through an Initial Public Offering("IPO") should disclose to the Audit Committee, the uses/applications of funds by major category (capital expenditure, sales and marketing, working capital, ate), on a quarterly basis.

9. It should be obligatory for the Board of a company to lay down the code of conduct for all Board members and senior management of a company. This code of conduct shall be posted on the website of the company. All Board members and senior management personnel shall affirm compliance with the code on an annual basis. The annual report of the company shall contain declaration to this effect signed off by the CEO and COO.

10. Where an institution wishes to appoint a director on the Board, such appointment should be made by the shareholders. There shall be no nominee directors.

11. All compensation paid to non-executive directors may be fixed by the Board of Directors and should be approved by shareholders in general meeting. Limit should be set for the maximum number of stock options that can be granted to non-executive directors in any financial year and in aggregate. The stock option granted to the non-executive directors shall vest after a period of at least one year from the date such non-executive directors have retired from the Board of the Company.

12. Personnel who observe an unethical or improper practice (not necessarily a violation of law) should be able to approach the audit committee without necessarily informing their supervisors.

13. Companies shall annually affirm that they have not denied any personnel access to the audit committee of the company (in respect of matters involving alleged misconduct) and that they have provided protection to 'whistle blowers' from unfair termination and other unfair or prejudicial employment practices. The appointment, removal and terms of remuneration of the chief internal auditor must be subject to review by the Audit Committee. Such affirmation shall form a part of the Board report on Corporate Governance that is required to be prepared and submitted together with the annual report.

14. The provisions relating to the composition of the Board of Directors of the holding company should be made applicable to the composition of the Board of Directors of subsidiary companies.

15. The performance evaluation of non-executive directors should be by a peer group comprising the entire Board of Directors, excluding the director being evaluated the peer group evaluation should be the mechanism to determine whether to extend/continue the terms of appointment of non-executive directors.

16. SEBI should make rules for the following:

    (a) Disclosure in the report issued by a security analyst whether the company that is being written about is client of the analysts employer or a associate of the analyst's employer and the nature of services rendered to such company, if any; and

    (b) Disclosure in the report issued by a security analyst whether the analyst or the analysts' employer or an associate of the analysts' employer hold or held (in the 12 months immediately preceding the date of the report) or intend to hold any debt or equity instrument in the issuer company that is the subject-matter of the report of the analyst.

Summary

The concept of Corporate Governance is a recent phenomenon. It started in an organized manner in 1990s and took off in the last decade of 21st century. The concept gathered momentum particularly during the nineties and other countries.

The prominence of Corporate Governance began in UK, with the Cadbury Committee, after various instances of business failure, fraud, lack of investor confidence in financial reporting and in the reports of auditors.

Even in the United States of America, a highly regulated and disciplined society, many giant companies such as Enron, WorldCom etc., have failed because of reported gross mis-management, couple with fraud committee by the top management. Questions have arisen thick and fast as to how people entrusted with Governance of these Corporates, not to speak of the statutory auditors, had failed to detect and stern the rot, before it was too late, many committees —The Cadbury Committee Report in UK (1992) and (1996), Hampel Committee Report in UK (1997), the OECD Principles (1998), the Blue Ribbon Committee Report in US (1998) and as many as five Committees on Corporate Governance in India, namely *(i)* Committee on Corporate Governance of CII 1992, *(ii)* Ganguly Committee of Reserve Bank of India, *(iii)* K.M.Birla Committee (SEBI), *(iv)* Murthy Committee (SEBI) 1993 and *(v)* Naresh Chandra Committee (Government of India) have examined these and many more vital aspects of Corporate Governance. All of them without exception suggested the constitution of at least Audit Committee for ensuring transparency in corporate accounts. In fact, the Cadbury Committee (UK) was the first to suggest creation of these strong pillars of Corporate Governance, in the form of these Committees such as (1) Nomination Committee; (2) Remuneration Committee and (3) Audit Committee.

In fact, all the Committees, both foreign and Indian, highlighted the critically and important of these Committees. The nomination committees, for example, play a vital role in selecting independent non-executive Directors to the Board. Similarly, the remuneration Committee decides the remuneration to be paid to the non-executive Directors and the audit committee ensures that the company accounts exhibit the true and fair position of the company's financial health.

REFERENCES

1. *Corporate Governance*—R.S. Raghavan Bank Economists Conference 2001, p. 439, Indian Banking.
2. *Corporate Governance in the Banking Sector— A Framework of Analysis*, Shri N.V. Rao, Bank Economists Conference 2001, p. 451, Indian Banking.
3. *Corporate Governance*—Sri G. Krishna Murthy, Bank Economists Conference 2001, p. No, 26, Indian Banking.
4. *Corporate Governance and Corporate Social Responsibility: Need for Indian Public Sector Banks*—Madhu Sehgal, Bank Economists Conference 2003, Indian Banking—Moving towards Globalisation, p. 132.
5. *Corporate Governance in Financial Sector* Inaugural address at the Workshop on Corporate Governance in Banks and Financial Institutions Administrative College of India, June 14, 1999, p. 59.
6. Corporate Governance for Regional Rural Banks—Dr. Krishore G.Padhy Bank Economists Conference 2001, p. 463, Indian Banking.
7. *A Governance Prescription for IT in Indian Banking Sector*—Dr. V. P. Gulati, Bankers Conference 2004, p. 323, Indian Banking: Realizing Global Aspirations.
8. *Corporate Governance—Perspective in Urban Co-operative Banks*—Dr. K. Shankar Shetty, Bank Economists Conference 2002, p. 179, Indian Banking: Managing Transformation.
9. *Consolidation and Restricting of Banks*—Mr. Sitarama Murthy, Bank Economists Conference 2001, p. 29, Indian Banking.
10. *Corporate Governance in Banks—Concepts and Issues*—Dr. K.M. Bhattacharya, Bank Economists Conference 2001, p. 458, Indian Banking: Paradigm Shift.
11. *Corporate Governance in Banking and Finance*—2000, Y.R.K. Reddy & Yerram Raju.
12. *Corporate Governance: Global Concepts and Practices*—Dr. S. Singh.

23

Corporate Governance and Business Ethics in India

Dr. K.S. Bose

Ethics and Social Responsibility are concepts that are fundamentally about the quality of our relationship over time. With the growing strength of consumer movements and rising levels of awareness among stakeholders, corporations are realizing that stakeholders and consumers are no longer indifferent to unethical practices like financial irregularities, tax-evasion, poor quality products and services, kick-backs, non-compliance with environmental issues, and hazardous working conditions. Many Indian companies too have recognized the importance of integrity, transparency and open communications. They believe that the goodwill resulting from adopting and successfully implementing a code of business ethics will, in the long run, translate into economic gains. Today, investors want to ensure that the companies they invest are not only managed properly, but also have proper corporate governance. They regard corporate governance as a control mechanism that ensures the optimum use of the human, physical and financial resources of an enterprise. Companies have now begun to integrate ethics into their corporate cultures and concentrate on putting appropriate corporate governance mechanisms in place.

Strong Corporate Governance is indispensable to a resilient and vibrant corporate market and is an important instrument of investor protection. It is the blood that fills the veins of transparent corporate disclosure and high quality accounting practices. The essence of corporate governance involves the development of a constructive relationship between different constituents of a corporate enterprise based on the principles of fairness, transparency and accountability. Such a mechanism enables corporations to attract monetary and human resources, enables Board to monitor the performance of the management, crucial for his assigned role of running the enterprise for the common benefit of all constituents. Economic resources would flow only to corporations having impeccable corporate governance credentials.

For the developing economies seeking to integrate with the global economy, corporate governance is of critical importance, as it is the key parameter used for evaluation by global investors or strategic partner. The fall of many US corporations in the early years of the 21st century brought one clear message to the fore: ethics matters in business. The public is perception of corporate ethics changed dramatically with the revelation of the unethical decision-making at WorldCom and Enron. The scandals took a toll on consumer's confidence and portfolios, and undermined their faith in the accounting profession. Corporate stakeholders have called for more transparent financial reporting and evidence of better ethical conduct.

Corporate governance is about commitment to values and ethical business conduct. It is about how an organization is managed. This includes its corporate and other structures, its culture, policies and the manner in which it deals with various stakeholders. Accordingly, timely and accurate disclosure of information regarding the financial situation, performance, ownership and governance of the company is an important part of corporate governance. This improves public understanding of the structure, activities and policies of the organization. Consequently, the organization is able to attract investors, and enhance the trust and confidence of the stakeholders.

Corporate Governance—Definition

Corporate governance has succeeded in attracting a good deal of public interest because of its apparent importance for the economic health of corporations and society in general. However, the concept of corporate governance is poorly defined because it potentially covers a large number of distinct economic phenomenon. As a result different people have come up with different definitions that basically reflect their special interest in the field. It is hard to see that this 'disorder' will be any different in the future so the best way to define the concept is perhaps to list a few of the different definitions rather than just mentioning one definition. A few are:

"Corporate governance is a field in economics that investigates how to secure/motivate efficient management of corporations by the use of incentive mechanisms, such as contracts, organizational designs and legislation. This is often limited to the question of improving financial performance, for example, how the corporate owners can secure/motivate that the corporate managers will deliver a competitive rate of return", *www.encycogov.com*, Mathiesen (2002).

"Corporate governance deals with the ways in which suppliers of finance to corporations assure themselves of getting a return on their investment", *The Journal of Finance*, Shleifer and Vishny (1997, p. 737).

"Corporate governance is the system by which business corporations are directed and controlled. The corporate governance structure specifies the distribution of rights and responsibilities among different participants in the corporation, such as, the board, managers, shareholders and other stakeholders, and spells out the rules and procedures for making decisions on corporate affairs. By doing this, it also provides the structure through which the company objectives are set, and the means of attaining those objectives and monitoring performance", OECD April 1999. OECD's definition is consistent with the one presented by Cadbury (1992, p. 15).

"Corporate governance—which can be defined narrowly as the relationship of a company to its shareholders or, more broadly, as its relationship to society -....", from an article in *Financial Times* [1997].

"Corporate governance is about promoting corporate fairness, transparency and accountability," J. Wolfensohn, president of the Word Bank, as quoted by an article in *Financial Times*, June 21, 1999.

Corporate Governance—Why?

In the process of implementing corporate governance practices, the private sector begins practicing the fundamentals of democracy and builds safeguards against corrupt practices on the part of both the business community and the government. At its core, corporate governance deals with issues that result from the separation of ownership and control. Frequently, the decision to invest in a particular profit-making firm is made from a distance by investors who are removed from the day- to- day operations of the company. But corporate governance goes beyond simply establishing a transparent and responsible relationship between managers and owners. The presence of strong corporate governance standards provides increased access to capital and thus aids economic development. For the past several decades, hardly any development efforts were successful without foreign investment. Good corporate governance attracts investors by assuring them that the business environment is fair and transparent; that companies can be held accountable for their actions or inactions; and that investments can be protected and contracts enforced. It is obvious that corporate governance is important for investors because it creates better-managed companies. Yet corporate governance is equally important for society, because the day-to-day practice of corporate governance standards requires that companies support the rule of law and efficient courts that uphold property rights. It requires that financial records be independently audited and that avenues of corruption be exposed. It requires that shareholders be given information so that they can make informed decisions. As corporate failures inevitably have negative effects on the society and governments, good corporate governance is in the best interest of all parties.

Business Ethics and Corporate Governance

Business ethics is the application of ethical values to business behaviour. It applies to any and all aspects of business conduct, from boardroom strategies and how companies treat their suppliers to sales techniques and accounting practices. Ethics goes beyond the legal requirements for a company and is, therefore, discretionary. Business ethics applies to the conduct of individuals and to the conduct of the organisation as a whole. It is about how a company does its business; how it behaves intrinsically. Corporate governance is meant to run companies ethically in a manner such that all stakeholders—creditors, distributors customers, employees, society at large and Governments are dealt in a fair manner. There was a belief at one time that the job of the management is to look after its shareholders alone. Now the whole concept of capitalism has changed and it has started adopting a much broader view for its own survival that is why it has now become important that governance should look at all stakeholders and not just shareholders. Corporate governance is not something, which regulators have to impose on a management but it should come from within. There is no point in making statutory provisions for enforcing ethical conduct.

Corporate Governance—History

Corporate Governance guidelines and best practices have evolved over a period of time. The Cadbury Report on the financial aspects of corporate governance, published in the United Kingdom in 1992, was a landmark. It led to the publication of the Viénot Report in France in 1995. This report boldly advocated the removal of cross-shareholdings that had formed the bedrock of French capitalism for decades. Further, The General Motors Board of Directors Guidelines in the United States and the Dey Report in Canada proved to be influential in the evolution of other guidelines and codes across the world. Over the past decade, various countries have issued recommendations for corporate governance. Compliance with these is generally not mandated by law, although codes that are linked to stock exchanges sometimes have a mandatory content.

The Sarbanes-Oxley Act, which was signed by the U.S. President George W. Bush into law in July 2002, has brought about sweeping changes in financial reporting. This is perceived to be the most significant change to federal securities law since the 1930s. Besides directors and auditors, the Act has also laid down new accountability standards for security analysts and legal counsels.

In November, 2003, the SEC approved changes to the NYSE and NASDAQ listing requirements. The changes focused mainly on Board independence, independent committees of the Board, audit committee composition, code of business conduct and ethics and related party transactions.

The Higgs Report on non-executive directors and the Smith Report on audit committees, both published in January 2003, form part of the systematic review of corporate governance being undertaken in the UK and Europe. This is in light of recent corporate failures.The recommendations of these two reports are aimed at strengthening the existing framework for corporate governance in the UK. Enhancing the effectiveness of the non-executive directors and switching the key audit relationship from executive directors to an independent audit committee are part of this. These recommendations are intended as revisions to the Combined Code on Corporate Governance.

In April 2004, the governments of the 30 Organisation for

Economic Co-operation and Development (OECD) countries approved a revised version of the OECD's Principles of Corporate Governance adding new recommendations for good practice in corporate behaviour with a view to rebuilding and maintaining public trust in companies and stock markets. The revised principles call on governments to ensure effective regulatory frameworks and on companies to be more accountable. The principles include increased awareness among institutional investors, enhanced role for shareholders in executive compensation, greater transparency and effective disclosures to counter conflicts of interest.

In India, the Confederation of Indian Industry (CII) took the lead in framing a desirable code of corporate governance in April 1998. This was followed by the recommendations of the Kumar Mangalam Birla Committee on Corporate Governance. This Committee was appointed by the Securities and Exchange Board of India (SEBI). The recommendations were accepted by SEBI in December 1999, and are now enshrined in Clause 49 of the Listing Agreement of every Indian stock exchange. SEBI also instituted a committee under the chairmanship of Mr. N. R. Narayana Murthy which recommended enhancements in corporate governance. SEBI has incorporated the recommendations made by the Narayana Murthy Committee on Corporate Governance in Clause 49 of the listing agreement.

In addition, the Department of Company Affairs, Government of India, constituted a nine-member committee under the chairmanship of Mr. Naresh Chandra, former Indian ambassador to the U.S., to examine various corporate governance issues. Our compliance with these recommendations is listed in the course of this report. We believe that sound corporate governance is critical to enhance and retain investor trust. Accordingly, we always seek to ensure that we attain our performance rules with integrity. Our Board exercises its fiduciary responsibilities in the widest sense of the term. Our disclosures always seek to attain the best practices in international corporate governance. We also endeavour to enhance long-term shareholder value and respect minority rights in all our business decisions.

Ethically Relevant Factors in Corporate Governance

This is not an exhaustive list of relevant factors. Furthermore, these factors are to some extent interconnected. The factors listed are largely covered by the Ethical Guidelines mentioned as given:

- The board's composition, qualifications and independence of senior management.
- The board and management's ability to look after shareholders' interests.
- Management remuneration systems (fixed salary, bonuses, options etc.).
- Internal control systems (supervision, audits etc.) and accountability mechanisms.
- Openness and transparency (including reporting systems).
- Labour standards (including workers' rights and health and safety).
- The company's approach to the environment.
- Business practice (including approach to legislation on corruption, taxation, competition, consumer rights, etc.).

Means of Influence in Corporate Governance

Corporate Governance work involves exerting a positive influence in companies in which it invests. Naturally, this applies not only to matters of an explicitly ethical nature but also more generally. This influence can be exerted in the following ways:

Communicating organization's ethical principles and guidelines: These principles and guidelines will be communicated to both partners on the investment side and companies in which investments are made.

Cooperating with other institutional investors: Influence over a company will be more effective if it is exerted by several investors in cooperation. Therefore, cooperate with other institutional investors, both formally and informally, with a view to forming a common front on important issues.

Voting at general meetings: Organization has to assess continuously how voting rights can be used to promote shareholder interests.

Contacting companies directly: If there are aspects of a company's board or management which come into conflict with the Fund's long-term profitability or its ethical principles in other ways, the organization has to discuss the matter directly with the company, primarily with its board. This may be done in cooperation with other investors.

Key elements of good corporate governance principles include honesty, trust and integrity, openness, performance orientation, responsibility and accountability, mutual respect, and commitment to the organisation. It is very important that, how directors and management develop a model of governance that aligns the values of the corporate participants and then evaluate this model periodically for its effectiveness. In particular, senior executives should conduct themselves honestly and ethically, especially concerning actual or apparent *conflicts of interest*, and disclosure in financial reports.

Commonly Accepted Principles of Corporate Governance

- *Rights and equitable treatment of shareholders:* Organisations should respect the rights of shareholders and help shareholders to exercise those rights. They can help shareholders exercise their rights by effectively communicating information that is understandable and accessible and encouraging shareholders to participate in general meetings.
- *Interests of other stakeholders:* Organisations should recognise that they have legal and other obligations to all legitimate stakeholders.
- *Role and responsibilities of the board:* The board needs a range of skills and understanding to be able to deal with various business issues and have the ability to review and challenge management performance. It needs to be of sufficient size and have an appropriate level of commitment to fulfill its responsibilities and duties. There are issues about the appropriate mix of executive and non-executive directors. The key roles of chairperson and CEO should not be held by the same person.
- *Integrity and ethical behaviour:* Organisations should develop a code of conduct for their directors and executives that promotes ethical and responsible decision-making. It is important to understand, though, that systemic reliance on

integrity and ethics is bound to eventual failure. Because of this, many organizations establish Compliance and Ethics Programmes to minimize the risk that the firm steps outside of ethical and legal boundaries.

- *Disclosure and transparency:* Organisations should clarify and make publicly known the roles and responsibilities of board and management to provide shareholders with a level of accountability. They should also implement procedures to independently verify and safeguard the integrity of the company's financial reporting. Disclosure of material matters concerning the organisation should be timely and balanced to ensure that all investors have access to clear, factual information.

Issues involving corporate governance principles include:

- oversight of the preparation of the entity's financial statements,
- internal controls and the independence of the entity's auditors,
- review of the compensation arrangements for the chief executive officer and other senior executives,
- the way in which individuals are nominated for positions on the board,
- the resources made available to directors in carrying out their duties,
- oversight and management of risk, and
- dividend policy.

Systemic Problems of Corporate Governance

- *Supply of accounting information:* Financial accounts form a crucial link in enabling providers of finance to monitor directors. Imperfections in the financial reporting process will cause imperfections in the effectiveness of corporate governance. This should, ideally, be corrected by the working of the external auditing process.
- *Demand for information:* A barrier to shareholders using good information is the cost of processing it, especially to a small shareholder. The traditional answer to this problem is the

efficient market hypothesis (in finance, the Efficient Market Hypothesis (EMH) asserts that financial markets are efficient), which suggests that the shareholder will free ride on the judgements of larger professional investors.

- *Monitoring costs:* In order to influence the directors, the shareholders must combine with others to form a significant voting group which can pose a real threat of carrying resolutions or appointing directors at a general meeting.

Commitment to Ethical Corporate Governance: Required Practices

1. *Ownership structure.* Provide a chart setting out the important shareholdings, holding companies, affiliates and subsidiaries of the company, indicating *ultimate beneficial* ownership and percentages of shares held by each.
2. *Governance structure.* Provide a chart setting out the governance structure of the company, indicating the principal organs of the company's governance and to whom each reports.
3. *Major transactions and material events.* Provide a timeline of major transactions and material events for the past five years (in particular, corporate acquisitions, mergers, restructurings and sales or purchases of major assets, etc.).
4. *Organic documents.* Please provide an English translation of the company's charter and other organic documents.
5. *Policies relating to corporate governance.* What written policies, codes or manuals have been elaborated that set out the company's approach to governance, the respective roles, responsibilities and composition of the Board, disclosure and transparency practices, and treatment of minority shareholders?
6. *Corporate events calendar.* Provide an annual calendar of corporate events, including Shareholders Meetings and Board's meetings?
7. *Company corporate governance code.* The company has to design Corporate Governance Code (or "Policy" or "Guidelines") that outlines the governance practices of the company and, in particular, the role of the Board? What are

the company's procedures for monitoring its compliance with the Corporate Governance code?

8. *Code of Ethics.* The company has to formulate code of ethics and should be communicated in proper manner.

9. *Compliance responsibility.* Is a Board member or senior manager explicitly charged with responsibility for ensuring that the company complies with the law, its charter and its policies regarding corporate governance (i.e., the role of the Board, transparency and disclosure, treatment of shareholders), and code of ethics?

10. *Shareholders agreements.* Provide the details and translations of any shareholders agreements or other informal arrangements among all or some shareholders.

11. *Succession planning.* Succession planning of the chief executive of the company should be written. How much longer does the current chief executive intend to remain in this position? Has a successor been identified and agreed upon by the family?

12. *Family tree and share ownership.* Provide a family tree and accompanying explanation indicating the name, residence, occupation, birth-date, and share ownership of each family member.

13. *Family-member employment.* The company should have a written policy concerning family-member employment and related human resources issues.

14. *Non-family share ownership.* The company should have a written policy concerning non-family share ownership.

Structure and Functioning of the Board of Directors

1. *Establishment of a Board of Directors.* The Company should have a Board of Directors, which meets according to a regular schedule.

2. *Board policies.* Provide English translations of any policies or by-laws relating to the Board of Directors.

3. *Agenda and minutes.* Agenda should be prepared and distributed in advance of Board meetings. And minutes should prepared and approved after the Board meetings.

4. *Current Board membership.* Provide a list of the current members of the Board with summary CVs indicating, at a minimum, their affiliations with the company, management and controlling shareholders, and other companies on which such persons sit as Board members.
5. *Composition of the Board.* Composition of the Board of Directors should be determined.
6. *Skill mix.* What sorts of business and other experience are represented on the Board? What efforts are made to ensure an appropriate mix of skills and experience among Board members?
7. *Functioning of the Board.* Does the Board of Directors serve the classic functions of a Board (providing guidance to and monitoring the performance of the senior management for the benefit of all shareholders) or is the Board's primary function to act as a meeting of shareholders or a meeting of senior family members?
8. *Board evaluation.* Does the Board conduct self-evaluations or other reviews of its effectiveness? How are such reviews conducted and with what frequency?
9. *The Board and the family.* What is understood as the role of the Board *vis-à-vis* the family?
10. *Advisory Board.* If the Board does not include outside members, or if no Board exists, does the company have an Advisory Board of independent professionals that is consulted on a regular basis? If such Advisory Board exists, who are its members and how were they selected?

Control Environment and Processes: Internal Control (IC), Internal Audit (IA) and External Audit (EA)

1. *Internal control design:* Please describe how the company's internal controls (operational, financial, and for the company's highly automated systems) are designed and maintained.
2. *Internal control assurance:* What is the role of the audit committee? Does the board periodically review the policies and procedures designed to ensure that proper internal

controls are instituted and maintained?

3. *Outsourcing of the internal audit function:* Please respond to the following questions if your IA function is outsourced. What is the company's policy with respect to the selection of IA service providers? Was the appointment of the provider reviewed by the audit committee? Are the outside service provider and its staff appropriately licensed?
4. *External audit and external auditors.* Are the annual financial statements audited by independent external auditors and approved by the shareholders' meeting? How are the external auditors selected? To whom, in form and in practice, are the external auditors responsible?
5. *Coordination between external and internal auditors.* Please respond to the following questions if the firm's accounts and internal controls are reviewed by external auditors. What is the procedure and calendar over the course of the fiscal year for interaction between the external and internal auditors?
6. *Reporting and internal controls:* Has the CFO or CEO reported to the board, audit committee and the external auditors all material IC weaknesses that may have impaired the reliability of the financial reports?
7. *Compliance Programme.* Please describe the company's compliance programme or procedures including training of employees, auditing and monitoring systems, company "hotline" for reporting violations and guidance as to conflicts of interest and appropriate sanctions and disciplinary action for violations. What information does the company provide to the shareholders regarding its compliance programme and its results?

Transparency and Disclosure

1. *Information dissemination.* Please summarize the company's policies and practices with respect to the preparation and dissemination of periodic financial and non-financial information about the company.
2. *Financial reports.* How often does the company prepare financial reports (quarterly, bi-annually, or annually)? Are

these reports approved by the Board?

3. *Review of the financial reports:* (Several of these questions are only relevant if the firm has an annual external audit; please answer the queries which are applicable.) Is the audit committee or board briefed on the major off-balance sheet items and their potential impact if taken into account on the financial statements?
4. *Shareholders agreements.* Are shareholders agreements with or among the controlling shareholders disclosed to all shareholders?
5. *Disclosure to interested parties.* How does the company ensure that all financial stakeholders of the same class (e.g., the controlling family, minority shareholders and lenders) are treated equally with respect to financial statements and other information on the company and have equal access to the same sets of accounts?

Index